Supporting the Development of Computer Science Concepts in Early Childhood

Supporting the Development of Computer Science Concepts in Early Childhood: A Practical Guide for Parents and Educators provides a solid understanding of computer science that sets your early childhood learner up for success!

The guide provides ways to introduce vocabulary, games to reinforce concepts, and printable activities that help early childhood learners understand computer science in an engaging, age-appropriate way.

This comprehensive guide covers the foundation of computer science (integrating the Computer Science Teachers Association K-2 standards) and includes information about binary, ciphers, using the command line, programming languages, sequencing, the basics of how computer systems and networks work, what hacking is, how to avoid phishing, and how to be a good digital citizen and stay safe online.

For effective use, this book should be purchased alongside the picture books *Little Hackers* and *Little Computer Scientists*. All three books can be purchased together as a set, *Developing Computer Science Concepts in Early Childhood* [978-1-032-47108-2].

Julie Darling is a teacher/librarian at the Ann Arbor STEAM school. She has a Master of Science in Information from the University of Michigan and is a Raspberry Pi certified educator. Julie has been teaching technology for more than 20 years.

D. J. Cools is a writer, illustrator, and designer with a passion for books, outdoor adventure, and old cars. Originally from Washington State, D. J. enjoys cycling, exploring, and small-town family life in Southeastern Michigan.

Supporting the Development of Computer Science Concepts in Early Childhood

A Practical Guide for Parents and Educators

Written by
Julie Darling

Illustrated by
D. J. Cools

Routledge
Taylor & Francis Group

NEW YORK AND LONDON

First published 2025
by Routledge
605 Third Avenue, New York, NY 10158

and by Routledge
4 Park Square, Milton Park, Abingdon, Oxon, OX14 4RN

Routledge is an imprint of the Taylor & Francis Group, an informa business

Library of Congress Cataloging-in-Publication Data
Names: Darling, Julie, author. | Cools, Darren, illustrator.
Title: Supporting the development of computer science concepts in early childhood: a practical guide for parents and educators / Julie Darling; [illustrated by Darren Cools].
Description: New York: Routledge, 2024. | For effective use, this book should be purchased alongside the picture books Little Hackers, and Little Computer Scientists. All three books can be purchased together as a set, Developing Computer Science Concepts in Early Childhood. | Includes bibliographical references.
Identifiers: LCCN 2024007048 (print) | LCCN 2024007049 (ebook) | ISBN 9781032471112 (pbk) | ISBN 9781003501503 (ebk)
Subjects: LCSH: Computer science–Study and teaching (Elementary)
Classification: LCC QA76.27 .D36 2024 (print) | LCC QA76.27 (ebook) | DDC 372.34–dc23/eng/20240314
LC record available at https://lccn.loc.gov/2024007048
LC ebook record available at https://lccn.loc.gov/2024007049

ISBN: 978-1-032-47111-2 (pbk)
ISBN: 978-1-003-50150-3 (ebk)

DOI: 10.4324/9781003501503

Typeset in Calibri
by Deanta Global Publishing Services, Chennai, India

Access the Support Material: www.routledge.com/9781032471112

To my family—thank you for taking this journey with me and for cheering me every step of the way.

Parents and educators—I hope this book provides you with a blueprint from which to launch a lifelong love of learning, exploring, and finding the joy and creativity that comes from playing and creating, with technology.

To my A2 STEAM students and colleagues—thank you for helping shape these books with your thoughtful input.

Julie Darling

Contents

Contents

Introduction: How to Use This Book

Supporting the Development of Computer Science Concepts in Early Childhood: A Practical Guide for Parents and Educators was written with kids ages 4–8 in mind; however, many of the activities are also effective with slightly older learners (up to age 10). The standards used in this book are the Computer Science Teachers Association (CSTA) Computer Science standards for grades K–2 (reproduced with permission). Extension activities are based upon the author's experience with teaching technology for more than 20 years. These activities can be utilized by kids who've already mastered the content and are excited for more.

If you're just starting out teaching **computer science** to your child or your students, consider using this book linearly. You could also choose to jump around based upon need or interest, using the table of contents to find the topic you want.

Consider pairing this guidebook with the companion picture books, *Little Computer Scientists* and *Little Hackers*, for read-alouds that introduce computer science concepts and vocabulary using fun stories and engaging pictures. You can find additional resources on my website: authorjuliedarling.com.

Acknowledgements

My deepest gratitude to all the hands, big and small, involved in making this book better than it would ever be without you. First, Bree, Willa, and Brad Darling for inspiring and supporting me throughout this writing adventure. Mark Lawrence, Paula Lawrence, Jan Gray, Emily Gray, Dan Gray, Chana Hawkins, Nate Hatt, Rachel Jensen, Kelly Parachek, Sharon Norris, Cathy Darling, Bob Darling, Kara Darling, Blake Darling, Paula Ortiz, Brian Darling, Pixie Sharp, Sarah Primeau, Adil Ali, and Michelle Bernhardt for being such great cheerleaders. William Lau for providing valuable insights and permission to use your excellent computer science coloring pages. Anne Fitzpatrick and Darren Cools for the pieces that made these books possible in the first place. My colleagues and friends (and friends of friends) for the beta reads, ideas, and feedback, specifically Nancy Gibson, Lisa Pham, James Luxon, Kelly Newton, Sarah Van Loo, SaTonya Thomas, Emily Bawol, Chad Bertelson, Joe Thomas, Jenna Garcia, Kate Stafford, Nancy Rosenbaum, Heather Cooper, Monica Jones, Sandy Aldrich, and Louis Devaney. Rebecca Collazo, Quinn Cowen, Shelley Strelluf, Katherine Laidler, Alex Andrews, and the fabulous team at Routledge/Taylor & Francis. Finally, my A2 STEAM @ Northside students. You all inspire me every day. I hope you like these books you helped to shape.

Chapter 1

Computing Systems

Introduction

Introducing kids to computing systems should be done thoughtfully, with tasks and activities that make your learners feel empowered and engaged. Consider creating "Tech Boss" name tents for your learners, and think about ways to facilitate a growth mindset. Set them up for success by explicitly teaching how to use a mouse or a touchpad and how to tell the difference between software and hardware. Teach your learners to be safe online *and* help them to feel confident with independent exploration and coding. Teach your learners the *Input/Output* song. Consider some of the robots and/or physical computing options to increase the fun, and start your learners off right. Teach them to troubleshoot with the help of "Troubleshooting Tasha". You'll find ideas and templates for all of this and more in Chapter 1. Use this chapter as a touchstone from which to help your learners launch a lifelong love of computers and technology. Note that although I'll often refer to learners (plural) throughout this text, the majority of the content can be used for one-on-one teaching, too.

Getting Started

When teaching little kids how to select appropriate software for tasks, you'll need to start with the basics. Defining software is a good first step. Keep it simple. Explain that software tells the computer what to do, just like grown-ups tell *kids* what to do. However, unlike kids, computers *have to do* what you tell them. They don't get bored, frustrated, or tired—they just follow instructions.

Script for Explaining Software

Explain to your learners that in a classroom, a teacher might tell you to raise your hand and wait until you're called on, before asking your question (have them practice raising their hands. "Yes! Just like that."). A grown-up at home might tell you that you need to brush your teeth before you go to bed (have them pretend to brush their teeth—"Don't forget your teeth in the back!"). Sometimes you don't want to raise your hand or brush your teeth, or maybe you just forget. Say: "Have you ever forgotten to raise your hand or forgotten to brush your teeth?" Allow some time for your learners to respond. "I have too! We're human and that's okay. We practice and get better at it, right?"

Explain: "Computers don't have any feelings about what they're told. They don't forget and they don't have to practice. They just follow instructions. With a computer, you get to act like you're the grown-up, and you get to tell it what you want it to do. *You* get to be the boss. Isn't that fun?! First, though, you have to learn *how* to boss the computer. You need to know what it can and can't do. A computer can only do what it's programmed to do." This is a good point at which to do a quick check for understanding. Ask your learners: "Does a computer know how to do everything?" They will likely yell out "no!" since you already gave them this answer. You can also ask for thumbs up for "yes", thumbs down for "no", or thumbs to the side if they "aren't sure".

DOI: 10.4324/9781003501503-1

TECH BOSS

_____

"Tech Boss" Name Tents

Consider making table tent name cards for your learners to use. Referring to your learner as a "Tech Boss" gives them a sense of ownership and allows them to realize that they're in charge of their device (instead of the other way around, even if it sometimes feels that way).

These table tents can also be used as a visual cue if your learners are working together and taking turns when using devices or robots. The learner whose turn it is to type or select options can have their "Tech Boss" table tent on display, and their partner can have their table tent face down. You could use a timer; five minutes may be a good amount of time, depending on the task and age of your learners. When the timer counts down to zero, the partners switch tasks and table tent positions.

Setting Your Learners Up for Success

Say: "Is it okay to make mistakes sometimes?" (Wait for your learners to answer in the affirmative). Ask: "Do you think I ever make any mistakes?" You could share a personal story about a (perhaps humorous) mistake you made and how you fixed it. Next ask: "What can we do if we make a mistake, or if we don't understand something right away?" Guide your learners in responses such as: we try again, we see what we can do to fix it, we get better with practice, we ask for help from a friend, parent, or teacher, etc.

Growth Mindset

Pointing out that it's okay to make mistakes, and that we get better with practice is part of modeling a "growth mindset" (Dweck, 2007). Developing a "growth mindset" (as opposed to a "fixed mindset") is a critical part of any type of learning and should be continuously encouraged:

> This growth mindset is based on the belief that your basic qualities are things you can cultivate through your efforts, your strategies, and help from others. Although people may differ in every which way—in their initial talents and aptitudes, interests, or temperaments—everyone can change and grow through application and experience.
>
> *(Dweck, 2007)*

In my classroom, I publicly point out when I make mistakes and model how to fix them. For example, when I click on the wrong link or button, I'll invite my learners to help me problem-solve. I'll say something like "Oops I clicked on the wrong link! What can I do to fix it?" I'll often share examples of when I wasn't great at something but got better with practice. For example, "Did you know that when I first started learning how to type, I only used my pointer fingers and I was SUPER slow? How do you think I got faster at typing?"

Teach Kids How to Use the Mouse and Touchpad

Ask: "Does anyone know how you open up this program? How do we make it start?" You'll need to demonstrate that they click on the **icon**. This may be a single or double click depending upon the device. Little kids will need practice with this. Have them practice with you by pretending to click with their pointer finger on a table. Pointer fingers lifted, tell your learners to "single click, click one time", then "double click, click two times quickly". Make it into a game where you have them tap their fingers once or twice each time you call either one out. Mix up the order in which you declare single or double clicks. Have your learners take turns calling out "single/double click" and having the other kids respond by "clicking" with their fingers on the table.

Once they feel confident with this, introduce right clicking. Young learners may still be figuring out how to tell their right from their left, so start by explaining the difference between their pointer finger and their ring finger. Say: "Your pointer finger is the left click, your middle finger is the right click." Add "right click" to your clicking practice game. If anyone is still struggling with which finger to use, you could have them trace their hand onto a piece of paper and label their pointer finger "left click" and their middle finger "right click" (or just "L" and "R").

Once your learners have mastered all of this, they could try it on an unplugged/disconnected mouse, and then finally with a connected mouse to open the program of their choice (hooray!) If your learners are using devices that have track/touch pads, they may need to practice right-clicking using both their middle and ring fingers together with a two-finger press. Make sure to **scaffold** this. Reinforce that on computers we call the pictures an "icon" or "**thumbnail**". Have your learners repeat that back to you: "What do we call this [point]? What else could we call it?"

Cursors Can Be a Surprise at First

Young learners often initially have trouble figuring out how to make the cursor move the way they want it to. Many devices for young learners have touch screens (which I would highly recommend starting with). When they first encounter a mouse, they may try to pick it up off the table to get the cursor to go to the top of the screen, and usually won't know what to do with the mouse to keep moving the cursor once they've reached the edge of their table. They won't know to pick the mouse up in the air, move it, and then set it back down again. If your learners are working on a touchpad, they will need to learn to pick up their fingers instead of the mouse.

You'll need to model this for them and have them practice, again with an unplugged mouse at first. This can be a game too. Say: "Forward, away from you means up!" and have them move their mouse forward while repeating back to you "up!"; "Back, toward you means down!" and have them move their mice back while saying "down!" Then you could call directions out randomly: "Up! Up! Right! Down! Left! Left again! How do you keep going left?" Observe to make sure they're "driving their mice" in the correct direction and spend a little more time on anything giving them trouble. Once your learners have mastered these skills, it's time to help them start exploring their devices.

This should also work with learners using a touchpad. You'll want to exaggerate how you're picking your finger up and placing it back on the touchpad (and point out when you're using two fingers) so they can understand what you're doing.

Computing Systems—Devices—Inclusion

> **CSTA K-2 Standard 1A-CS-01:** Select and operate appropriate software to perform a variety of tasks, and recognize that users have different needs and preferences for the technology they use.
>
> *"People use computing devices to perform a variety of tasks accurately and quickly. Students should be able to select the appropriate app/program to use for tasks they are required to complete. For example, if students are asked to draw a picture, they should be able to open and use a drawing app/program to complete this task, or if they are asked to create a presentation, they should be able to open and use presentation software. In addition, with teacher guidance, students should compare and discuss preferences for software with the same primary functionality. Students could compare different web browsers or word processing, presentation, or drawing programs."*

Script for Exploring Programs and Apps

Say: "How do we know what your device can do?" This is going to elicit a variety of responses, many of which could be correct. You'll need to guide this conversation. The specific details will vary depending upon what kind of devices your learners have access to.

Point out that the software accessible in the dock, or on the desktop, isn't *everything* on the device. Show your learners how to find the programs/apps on their devices. If you're teaching your child one-on-one, you could sit next to them and point out how they find the software/apps loaded on their device. If you're on a Mac, one method you can use is to select Finder–Applications. On a PC, you'll likely go to Start–Settings–Apps. On an iPad, you'll go to the home screen and swipe until you get to the App Library. If you're instructing a class, it's useful to display the device on a big screen (you may need a document camera to do this), so that your learners can see what you're doing.

Ask: "What do you think all of these apps do? Is there a way to tell?" Point out that the programs/apps have pictures, called icons or thumbnails, and that on most devices when you "**mouse over**" (bring your cursor on top of, but don't click—this is sometimes also called "mouse hover") the programs/apps, writing usually appears. This written description gives you a little more information about what that program/app does.

Point out an intuitive example, the musical note for a music app is a good one. But what if you still can't tell what the program does after mousing over the icon? In order to learn more about programs/apps, that your grown-ups have told you are okay to use, you may need to open them.

Teaching kids how to independently explore their devices and use the correct terminology gives them confidence. This leads to mastery which in turn piques their interest in learning more. Teach kids to use computers for creating. Give them some choices of which apps/programs to use. Provide them with a few examples of what they could create using these apps/programs, to help them succeed.

Safety First

It's also important to teach your learners to explore safely. Talk with them about what to do if they encounter anything that's scary or makes them feel worried. Common Sense Education (www.commonsense.org/education) has great, free resources that can be used to facilitate productive, age-appropriate discussions about this. The most important takeaways are that your learners should never tell strangers online information about themselves (name, address, phone number, school they attend), and they should immediately get a trusted adult if they encounter anything that makes them feel uncomfortable, scared, or worried.

I'll often ask my students, "Would you walk up to a stranger in a park and tell them your name, address and phone number?" They know not to do this, so I'll continue by asking, "What about someone who messages you online?" Often, I'll need to clarify that it's okay for your grown-ups to give your address to a friend for a play date, but that it's super important to remember that it's your *grown-up* who's giving this address to someone. Kids should never give this information out without asking their grown-ups first.

Selecting Programs and Apps

Now that your learners have some idea of the programs/apps on their devices, and basic guidance about online safety, it's time to teach them how to select a program/app based upon the task they're trying to accomplish. Start by giving them a tour of their device and pointing out which app/program they would use for which task. "If I want to create a digital drawing, which of these apps would I choose? What if I want to write a story? How about if I want to learn to **code**? What if I just want to know what the weather is like outside today?"

Make sure to point out that different programs/apps can be used to accomplish similar tasks. Ask: "Why might someone choose one over another?" Point out that some programs/apps are web-based and therefore need the Internet to work. So, what do you do if you don't have access to the Internet or if your Internet tends to be spotty? That would be a good reason to use the program/app that *isn't* web-based. Maybe you just like one of them better; if they do basically the same task, would that be an okay reason to choose one app over another? Absolutely!

Software Extension: Explaining Operating Systems

When determining if software is compatible with (works with) your device, the first consideration is which **operating system** your device is running. The operating system's job is to manage all of the software and hardware running on your device. The three most commonly used operating systems are Microsoft Windows (most PCs), MacOS (Apple products), and Linux (**open source**). Use the *Operating Systems* coloring page on the next page to introduce operating systems to your learners.

Operating Systems

Every device needs an operating system in order to run. It's the most important piece of software on your device.

The three most common types of operating systems are Microsoft Windows, MacOS, and Linux.

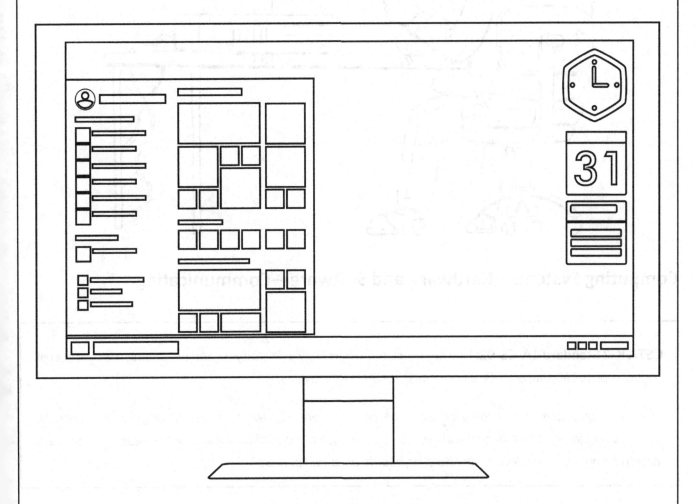

Image taken from *Computer Science Colouring Book: A gentle and fun introduction to Computer Science* by William Lau (reproduced with permission).

Computing Systems—Hardware and Software—Communicating

CSTA K-2 Standard 1A-CS-02: Use appropriate terminology in identifying and describing the function of common physical components of computing systems (hardware).

"A computing system is composed of hardware and software. Hardware consists of physical components. Students should be able to identify and describe the function of external hardware, such as desktop computers, laptop computers, tablet devices, monitors, keyboards, mice, and printers."

Teaching kids about hardware is important, but simply having them memorize facts is too dry. It's important to take this slowly. Allow kids to physically handle the items when possible and use games, songs, and humor to make learning more engaging.

Scripts for Teaching Hardware

Computer Mouse

Start by showing your learners an external, corded mouse. Say: "Does anyone know what this is called? Look, it has a tail! But in this case, since it connects to a computer, this part [point at the cord], is actually called a cord." If your learners don't guess correctly, explain that it's a computer mouse. Have them repeat back "computer mouse".

Give it a gentle tap with your finger. Ask: "Does this seem hard or soft?" Let them handle it to see that it's hard. Pass it around. Once everyone has had a chance to touch it, ask: "Do you think it's *hard*ware or *soft*ware?" Next ask: "What do I use this for?" If your teaching style is to be a little silly, you could say something like "Do I wear it as a hat? Do I use it as a belt? How about an earring? No?"

After you've had a laugh with your learners, bring it back to the lesson: "What *do* I use this for, then (if not as a fashion accessory)?" Explain that a computer mouse is like an extension of your finger or your hand. Mice are especially useful if you're not using a device with a touch screen. If you haven't played the mouse/cursor games from earlier in this chapter, explain that when you move your mouse along a flat surface, the pointer on the screen of your device moves in the same direction. When you tap (click) on the top, left side of your mouse, it clicks on the screen. If you click on the right side of your mouse, it often gives you extra options. If you *have* played the mouse/cursor games, you can invite a learner to demonstrate how mice work!

Desktop vs. Laptop Computers

When teaching your learners the difference between desktop and laptop computers, it's useful to have an example of at least one of each kind in the room. Say: "I have two (or however many) computers here." Tap on the side of each one. "Is this hard or soft? Does that make these computers *hard*ware?" (Yes!)

Differentiate between laptop and desktop computers by saying: "One of these is a laptop computer (point), one of these is a desktop computer (point). Which do you think would be more comfortable on my lap?" Have your learners point. "This smaller one here, right? It's a laptop computer, because I can put it on *top* of my *lap* to use it. Which one is better left on the desk?" Have your learners point. "This heavier one (possibly with more parts, depending on the type of computer) right? I'm going to leave that one on the *top* of my *desk* when I'm using it. It would be really uncomfortable on my lap! That's why it's called a *desktop* computer because you're going to want to keep it on your desk when you use it!"

Printer

Tap on the side of a printer (your learners should be getting used to this by now). Say: "Does this seem hard or soft?" Ask: "Does that make it hardware?" (Yes!) Ask: "What is this?" (A printer.) "What does it do?" (Prints documents when you "tell" it to.) Explain that some printers only print in black and white, while others can *also* print in color. Point out that printers are only built to handle certain sizes of paper. A running theme you should keep coming back to is that everything in computer science is defined by the ways in which hardware and software are built and programmed. These are their limitations. You could ask: "Could I build a printer that printed really big sheets of paper—giant posters, for example?" (Sure!) "Can this printer do that?" (No, because it wasn't built to do that.)

If you wanted to extend this lesson with older learners, you could follow up by asking: "Is there a way we could add parts or change pieces of this printer so it *could* print giant posters?" If yes, this is an aspect of hacking, making a device or program do something that it wasn't initially designed to do.

Monitors

Tap on the side of a monitor. Say: "Does this seem hard or soft?" Ask: "Does that make it hardware?" (Yes!) Ask: "What is this?" (A computer monitor/screen.) Explain: "A computer monitor is the screen that shows you what you're working on, and allows you to see what you can do with this computer."

If you're working with slightly older or more advanced learners, you can continue: "What you can use this computer for is limited by the software loaded onto it. Can you put additional software on this device by downloading/installing software/applications? Absolutely! Can you delete applications/software that are already installed? Yep! You can do that too. However, you should make sure you're not deleting something important or installing something that could have **malware**, especially if the computer doesn't belong to you. Can I add more monitors, so I have more space to see what I'm working on with my computer? Yes!"

If you've been following these scripts straight through, that's a lot of listening for younger learners. Depending on the age of your learners, consider breaking up the scripts into one new idea per day. Follow that up with a brain break, a song, or a game that will allow your learners to move. The *Input/Output Hokey Pokey* is a good choice because it connects to learning about hardware and software.

Input/Output Hokey Pokey

Sing these lyrics to the tune of the classic children's song *The Hokey Pokey*:

> You plug your mouse in [pretend to plug it in]
> You plug your keyboard in [pretend to plug it in]
> You type the words in [pretend to type]
> And you flex your hands about [open and close your hands]
> You do the input/output and you boss your tech around [turn around in place]
> That's what it's all about! [clap three times in rhythm with your words]
>
> You plug your printer in [pretend to plug it in]
> You print your words out [pretend to grab paper]
> You print your picture out [pretend you're holding documents in each hand]
> And you show them all about! [hold your pretend documents up]
> You do the input/output and you boss your tech around [turn around in place as you're saying this line]
> That's what it's all about! [clap three times]
>
> You do the innn-put, output [sway in place]
> You do the innn-put, output [sway in place]
> You do the innn-put, output [sway in place]
> That's what it's all about! [clap three times]

Extension—Physical Computing and Robots

The term **physical computing** is sometimes used interchangeably with robotics as both can include devices with sensors, lights, displays, motors, and other inputs/outputs. Such features make these devices incredibly engaging, and they're a great way to enhance your computer **STEAM** or **STEM** curriculum.

I've loosely separated the two for practicality; most of what's listed under "robots" is a self-contained unit, while the products listed under "physical computing" have multiple pieces that can be added and/or assembled as desired. I've also included a few options for advanced/older learners, for some ideas about where to go next. If you work in a school and you don't have funding for these through your organization, consider writing a grant. In my current school, my colleagues have had great success with the Bosch Best Grant (www.besteachergrant.org).

Physical computing and robotics encompass a variety of devices created for a range of ages, with an assortment of capabilities and price points. It can be a bit overwhelming. Make sure to do some research (hands on, if possible) before purchasing, and if you work in a school, consider just purchasing one before committing to a whole class set. This single device or kit could be used as a choice/station until you've determined what would work best in your space and with your age group. Below you'll find a brief overview of some good choices currently on the market.

Robots/Robotics Overview

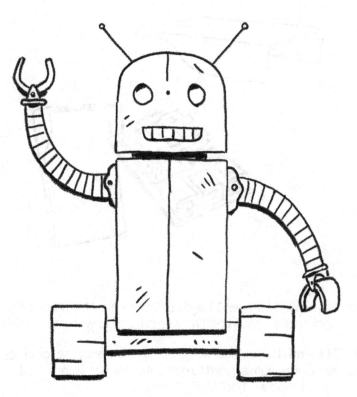

Bee-Bot/Blue-Bot ($$$) recommended for ages 3–8. Can be used screen-free. New models of Bee-Bot and all models of Blue-Bot include "see and say" (voice and perception).

Botley ($) recommended for ages 5 and up. Screen-free, you don't need additional devices to make it work, just the remote "transmitter". Includes an activity set.

Code & Go Robot Mouse ($) recommended for ages 4 and up. Code without screens using double-sided coding cards.

Edison Robot ($$) recommended for ages 4–16. Robot car. Can be coded using an age/skill progression from barcodes (for youngest learners) to "Edblocks", "EdScratch", and finally "EdPy".

Ozobot Evo ($$–$$$) recommended for ages 5 and up. Can be programmed using colored lines (color codes) or block-based programming (Ozoblockly). Can be used with or without screens.

Sphero Bolt ($$$) recommended for ages 8 and up (can be used with younger kids). Colorful, programmable robot ball. Bigger and with more features than the Sphero mini.

Sphero Mini ($$) recommended for ages 8 and up (can be used with younger kids). Colorful, programmable robot ball.

Wonder Workshop Dash ($$$) recommended for ages 6–11. Uses Blockly.

Physical Computing Overview

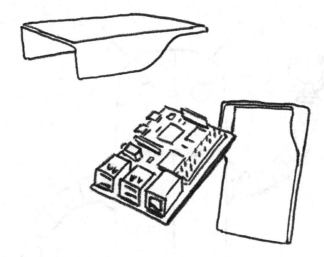

Arduino ($$–$$$) kits recommended for ages 11 and up. Can be used for advanced kids and more sophisticated projects. The kits include a variety of parts. A good next step for a kid who enjoyed Makey Makey.

LEGO® Education Spike™ Essential ($$$$) kits designed for classroom use for grades 1–5. Recommendation of one kit for every two learners. Curriculum aligned to computer science standards. LEGO® also has lessons/kits for PreK–K (Coding Express) and middle school (Spike™ Prime).

Makey Makey ($$) recommended for ages 8 and up. STEM "invention kit". Uses alligator clips to connect to conductive objects in the real world (your body, bananas, and more).

Micro:bit ($) recommended for ages 8–14. Compatible with Microsoft MakeCode, Python, and Scratch.

Raspberry Pi ($$–$$$) Can be used for advanced kids and more sophisticated projects. The kits include a variety of parts. A good next step for a kid who enjoyed Makey Makey. Similar to Arduino, but has its own operating system.

VEX ($$$–$$$$) has a variety of products with a range of prices. "123" is recommended for K and up, "GO" for Grades 3 and up, and "IQ" for grades 6 and up. The kits are versatile. They are designed for classroom use.

A Note About Ways to Learn to Code

The physical computing/robot choices can be used to learn different ways of **coding**. It may seem complex at first, but essentially there are three different ways to learn about coding that form a progression: (1) adaptations for emergent readers, (2) block-based coding, and (3) text-based coding.

Adaptations for Emergent Readers

My first recommendation is the ScratchJr app, which offers useful visual adaptations for **emergent readers** by teaching the concepts of coding with drag and drop, jigsaw-style puzzle pieces. Additional early childhood products (described in the *Robots/Robotics Overview* section) use features such as commands using your voice, cards, or colored lines. These allow our youngest learners to be successful as they're also learning to read.

Block-based Coding

Block-based coding options include **Scratch**, **Blockly**, and **Snap!** These also allow students to drag and drop jigsaw-style blocks of code which teach the principles of coding. Additionally, they include written details/instructions. Block-based coding is recommended as a first step for learning how to code (starting around ages 7 or 8 and up) for learners who can also read independently.

Text-based Coding

Text-based coding is for learners who already understand the basic principles of coding. Text-based coding involves typing the text commands of the actual programming language. The age at which learners are ready for this depends upon prior knowledge and motivation. This could be as early as age 8, depending on which programming language your learners are attempting to master and how much prior exposure to coding content they've had. **Python** and **HTML/CSS** are considered good ways to start. In contrast, I would not recommend starting with C++.

Computing Systems—Troubleshooting—Testing, Communicating

CSTA K-2 Standard 1A-CS-03: Describe basic hardware and software problems using accurate terminology.

"Problems with computing systems have different causes. Students at this level do not need to understand those causes, but they should be able to communicate a problem with accurate terminology (e.g., when an app or program is not working as expected, a device will not turn on, the sound does not work, etc.). Ideally, students would be able to use simple troubleshooting strategies, including turning a device off and on to reboot it, closing and reopening an app, turning on speakers, or plugging in headphones. These are, however, not specified in the standard, because these problems may not occur."

If your learners are anything like mine, when something goes wrong with their device, they start by saying it's "glitching" (or some similar catch-all phrase). "Glitch" is a useful word to indicate that something is going wrong. However, the first step for teaching kids how to successfully troubleshoot is to get them to be specific when describing the problem. The Troubleshooting Tasha to the Rescue handout on the following page includes useful steps for guiding troubleshooting (led by our mascot Troubleshooting Tasha). Consider using this as a tool to help **scaffold** troubleshooting with your learners.

Troubleshooting Tasha to the Rescue!

TROUBLE-SHOOTING TASHA

Troubleshooting Tasha is here to help fix your device! But *first* she needs to know the answer to these questions:

Question 1: *What* isn't working?

Question 2: *When* isn't it working (all the time or just on this one site/app/situation)?

Question 3: What can we do to try to fix it?

With some practice – you too can become a Troubleshooting Superhero!

Use this space to draw yourself wearing a cape while fixing your device.

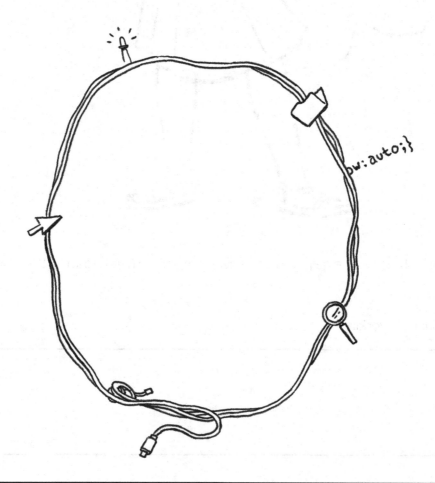

Conclusion

Chapter 1 contains everything you need to start your learners off on their computer science adventure in a thoughtful and joyful way. Continue to use the tools contained in this chapter to assist your learners as they progress with their knowledge of software, hardware, troubleshooting, coding, robotics, and physical computing. Peruse the *Resources* section in the back of this book for additional recommended materials.

References

Dweck, C. S. (2007). *Mindset: The New Psychology of Success*. Ballantine Books.

Lau, W. (2020). *Computer Science Colouring Book: A Gentle and Fun Introduction to Computer Science*. William Lau.

Chapter 2

Networks and the Internet

Introduction

Young learners are trusting by nature. They need to be taught when and how to be cautious. When introducing login credentials, you'll need to first teach your learners what a username and password *is* (a.k.a. login credentials). Be sure to follow that by explaining why we use these and who they should (and shouldn't) share them with. Use the handout *Login Credentials: Check for Understanding* with your older learners. Play *Click! Click! Malware* and the *Red Light/Green Light: Password Security Game* to make it fun. Sing *The Silly Password Song* together. Convey a basic understanding of how networking works, with *The Cloud Coloring Page*.

Networks and the Internet—Cybersecurity—Communicating

CSTA K-2 Standard 1A-NI-04: Explain what passwords are and why we use them, and use strong passwords to protect devices and information from unauthorized access.

"Learning to protect one's device or information from unwanted use by others is an essential first step in learning about cybersecurity. Students are not required to use multiple strong passwords. They should appropriately use and protect the passwords they are required to use."

Script for Teaching Login Credentials

Explain that a username is the way you tell a device (or app/website) that it's *you*. It connects you to *your* stuff (saved documents, email, saved games, and more). Your username usually doesn't change. A username is your special tech name. For safety, it should not be the same as your real name. Make sure your learners know that your username is okay to share with some people, but to check with a trusted adult first.

Explain that your password is the second part of accessing your device (or app/website) and it should be *extra* secret. Have your learners come up with some ideas for why they think this is important. I usually take some time to explain that if someone has your password, they can get into your stuff and mess around with it. Just like it's not fun if someone goes into your room and messes up your stuff, it's also not fun when someone gets into your stuff on your device and messes it up. We want to avoid that.

DOI: 10.4324/9781003501503-2

"Your password is between you, your device, and your trusted grown-ups." Pause here and review who *is* and *isn't* a trusted grown-up. "Is your teacher a trusted grown-up? How about your neighbor? Your best friend? What about your grown-ups at home? Does your teacher need to know your username and password for a computer that you use at home? (No). Does your grown-up at home need to know about your username and password for school devices? (Yes, especially if you bring these home to do homework)." You may want to review this a few times so that they get the hang of it. If your style is to be silly, you could also ask if your dog, cat, bird, or the squirrel outside the window need to know your login credentials.

Red Light/Green Light: Password Security Game

Play the Red Light/Green Light game, and use it to reinforce when to keep passwords safe. In the traditional game, one person stands on one side of a space such as a gym, field, or playground (the "caller") and everyone else is on the other side. When the caller says "green light!" everyone runs toward them, trying to reach them first. When the caller says "red light!" everyone has to stop. Anyone who does not stop quickly enough (or runs when they hear "red light!") has to go back to the starting point. You can call "green light" or "red light" consecutively to mix things up. The person who reaches the caller first gets to become the new caller.

To use this game to teach kids when it's okay to share passwords, instead of yelling out "red light!" and "green light!" yell out the names/titles of people that *should* or should *not* know a kid's password. You could have a list (images and written words) for the caller to use, with columns and/or green or red text to help indicate who *is* and is *not* a safe person to share passwords with. Names and titles can be reused within the same game, if need be.

Some "red light" examples could be: your neighbor, your friend, your cousin, a stranger, someone you just met. Some "green light" examples could be: your teacher, your school librarian, your grown-ups, your guardian, your dog, your cat, yourself. Talk through which answers are "red" and "green" with your learners in advance of the game and make sure to tailor this to your community. With my younger learners, I always use the term "grown-ups" to talk about their trusted adults at home since not all of my students live with a mom and dad, and "grown-ups" is more inclusive. With my older learners, I say "trusted adult" for the same reason.

Again, you could add various animals to make it silly, as long as you tell your learners in advance which category these animals are in (a bird that can repeat passwords back isn't a good animal to share your password with, but any other animal could be a "green light").

Tell your learners that, unlike your username, your password *should* change from time to time. It should also be changed *right away* if someone who is *not* a trusted adult uses it (such as another kid). When teaching older learners, I elaborate that sometimes you might get a message (usually an email) that someone else may have accessed your account. This is another situation when changing your password and maybe enabling **multi-factor authentication** is an important action to take. When multi-factor authentication is enabled, the first "factor" is your password, but another "factor" is required, such as a verification code that was texted or emailed to you, or biometrics such as voice, fingerprint, face or retina scan, etc. If you're pretty confident that you're the only one using your login credentials, your password should *still* be changed every once in a while. *Just in case*. For younger learners, once a year should be sufficient.

If your learners have never used their own username and password when logging in, they'll need lots of practice. Their usernames should never be more than eight characters and their passwords should also be simple. A good rule of thumb for younger learners is to create passwords that are two words, together, with a capital letter in the middle and a single digit number at the end—for example, "techBoss1". They'll need practice figuring out how to create a capital letter and where to find the numbers and letters on their keyboards. However, using a password that includes capital letters and numbers helps to teach young learners the basis for creating secure passwords. As they get older, they can add a symbol.

By limiting the number of characters your younger learners need to use, you'll increase their chances of mastering the skill of logging in independently. Security and usability should always be in balance when considering login credentials for young learners. In a school setting, I would strongly recommend creating a login card for each of your learners, with their names on the front of the card and their login credentials on the back. Point out that they should flip the cards back over (so just their names are showing) when they don't need them for logging in. This is another way to reinforce keeping login credentials secure.

In a school setting, when you're first teaching your learners to log in, consider also creating a handout with screenshots that they can look at as they move through the steps. Leave extra time for practice and have other

activities ready for your learners who are faster at completing this task. With younger learners, consider using songs to help them remember to keep their passwords safe such as *The Silly Password Song*.

The Silly Password Song

Keep your password safe. Shh Shh Shhhhh [hold finger to lips]
Keep your password safe! Shh Shh Shhhhh [hold finger to lips]
Don't tell your brother
Don't tell each other
Keep your password safe! Shh Shh Shhhhh [hold finger to lips]

Make your password long [stretch your arms out]
Make your password long [stretch your arms out]
Make your password long [stretch arms] to make it strong [bicep curl]
Make your password long [stretch your arms out]
Keep your password safe. Shh Shh Shhhhh [hold finger to lips]

Change your password a lot [stretch your fingers out and move them like you're typing]
Change your password a lot [stretch your fingers out and move them like you're typing]
Change your password a lot, don't let it get caught! [act like you're snatching something out of the air]
Change your password a lot [stretch your fingers out and move them like you're typing]
Keep your password safe. Shh Shh Shhhhh [hold finger to lips]

Cybersecurity Extension: More Secure Passwords

Figure 2.1   An example of a secure password.

If you're working with older kids, teach them that a secure password is a password that is long (the longer the better) and contains a combination of letters (capital and lower-case), numbers, and symbols. In addition, your password is much more secure if unique passwords are used for each account (and unique usernames too, when possible). You should avoid using easily guessable information such as birth dates, family or pet names, or the word "password".

Having said that, a secure password also needs to be one you can remember. Current best practice recommends 3–4 random words and a symbol. This is much easier to recall, making people less likely to write down their passwords in easily discoverable places.

Another good rule of thumb is to substitute out some letters for numbers or symbols. If you do this consistently, it's easy to remember. For example, replacing the letter O with a zero (0) or a letter S with a dollar sign ($) will make the password more secure. Using this format, I could write "less is more" like this: le$$i$m0re.

An additional recommendation (when possible) is to create unique passwords for each login and keep them safe in a password manager such as PassKeep. Password managers save your login credentials, making them secure and eliminating the need for memorization (although you'll still need to memorize the one you use to access the password manager).

Not following these tips makes your password more susceptible to a brute-force attack. An example of a **brute-force attack** is when a **black hat hacker** attempts to gain access to your account by trying every possible password combination. If your password is short (e.g., a four-digit number) or a word found in a dictionary, it's more vulnerable to brute-force attacks.

Login Credentials: Check for Understanding

Name:

_____

What is a username?

_____

What is a password?

_____

Why do we keep our passwords secret?

_____

Who should we keep them secret from?

_____

Can your grown-ups know your passwords?

_____

How do you create a secure password (that you can remember)?

_____

Cybersecurity Extension: Using Games

Once your learners understand the basics, you'll want to progress with more information about **cybersecurity** and Internet safety. Research shows that using games and songs and reinforcing content in different ways (showing, telling, and adding movement) helps kids to remember more of what they learn. Even with more serious topics, do your best to engage with the material in fun ways whenever possible. Consider the *Click Click Malware!* Game.

Click Click Malware!

Use the traditional children's game Duck Duck Goose to reinforce that clicking on an unknown website can cause your computer to get infected with malware. Just as in the traditional game, have your learners sit in a circle with their bodies facing in toward each other.

The designated "mouse" (who could wear mouse ears) will tap each kid gently on the head. In this way, they will "click" (tap) each "website" (kid's head). Instead of saying "duck" or "goose" with each tap (as in the traditional game), the mouse will say "click" or "malware".

When the mouse taps a kid's head and says "malware", that kid will jump up and try to tag/infect the mouse (computer), and the mouse will try to run around the circle of kids and sit in the malware's spot...before getting tagged. If the mouse makes it back to the spot without getting tagged, they're "safe" (they could yell out "virus quarantined" or "anti-virus software worked") and the malware gets to switch roles and act as the mouse. If the original mouse does *not* make it to the open/safe spot before getting tagged, they have to start over as the mouse and try again. With older learners, instead of just "malware", they could name specific types of **malware**: **virus**, **worm**, **spyware**, **ransomware**, etc.

Cybersecurity Extension: Introducing Vocabulary

In order for kids to understand more about any subject, they need to understand the terminology used. This is part of the intent of the companion picture books *Little Computer Scientists* and *Little Hackers*. As your learners progress, explain the following.

When your computer has malware (virus, spyware, worm), you may be able to fix the issue by **rebooting** your computer using **safe-mode.** This means that you would restart the computer in such a way that you're only running the most basic programs your computer needs to run. This way of restarting your device helps you to identify and fix potential problems (which includes but isn't limited to malware). In order to figure out how to reboot using safe-mode on your device, Google "reboot", "safe-mode", and your specific type of device (e.g., "Macbook Air").

A **quarantined virus** is a virus that has been confined to a safe area where it can't infect the rest of your device. You do this using anti-virus software. A **Trojan Horse**, named after the ancient Greek story about the fall of the City of Troy, is when malware is disguised as a legitimate program. Once downloaded, the malware causes harm. This is another type of virus that can be quarantined using anti-virus software. Some examples of currently recommended (as of the writing of this book) anti-virus software are Avira, McAfee, Bitdefender, Malwarebytes, and Norton Antivirus.

Speaking of hacking, **hackers** aren't always up to no good. There are three categories of hacking: white hat, gray hat, and black hat. **White hat hacking** is what cybersecurity experts do. They work to find and fix vulnerabilities and try to prevent other hackers from getting in. This is also referred to as "ethical hacking". Launching a fake cyberattack to find vulnerabilities is called **penetration testing** or "pen testing" for short. **Gray hat hacking** is when someone hacks into systems (without permission), in order to raise awareness and expose vulnerabilities (this is also called hacktivism). **Black hat hacking** is when someone hacks into a system (without permission) with the intent to do damage and/or steal information.

Extension—Networking—Some Basics

In *Little Computer Scientists*, the friends set up a **LAN** (local area network), so that they can all build together in Minecraft. A common use for a LAN is the devices linked through **Wi-Fi** in your house. Another example is in school: computers and printers are part of the network so that files can be shared easily, and everyone can access the printers. Networked devices can be super convenient and fun. However, as with many things that are fun, they can also pose a security risk. For example, if someone accesses the network where your devices are all linked together, they now could potentially hack into all these linked devices. This is why we use firewalls and sometimes secure routers and switches to make hacking less likely (and why you need to be extra careful when using public, password-free Wi-Fi).

The Internet itself is also considered a network. This network is often called "**the cloud**". Use *The Cloud Coloring Page* to show your learners the kinds of devices that could be connected to the cloud.

The Cloud

The objects drawn below can all connect to the Internet. That's why they're called the **Internet of Things** (or IOT for short).

The Internet is the biggest network in the world. It's often called **the cloud** (although you can't see it with your eyes—you have to imagine what it looks like). Using the cloud to access or control these objects is called **cloud computing**. You can imagine it like a big cloud floating above your head with all the objects— the Internet of Things—connecting to it.

Color in the objects you recognize. Next, color the cloud however you imagine it.

Count the number of objects you recognize. Write that number here: ____

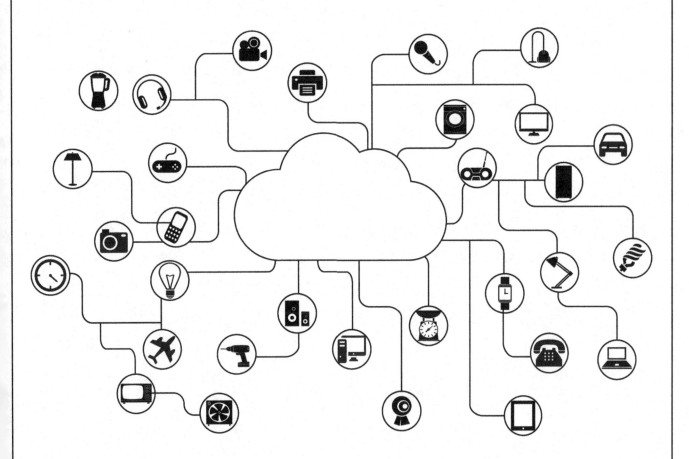

(Coloring page from *Computer Science Colouring Book* by William Lau. Reproduced with permission.)

Conclusion

Networking and cybersecurity are nuanced and ever-evolving subjects, so it's helpful to teach these using broad strokes. For young learners, gently introducing the concept of security, and why it's necessary, is sufficient. Networking and cybersecurity jobs continue to be in high demand; learners who find these topics interesting should be encouraged to continue exploring these. I hope you've enjoyed playing *Click Click Malware!* and *The Red Light/Green Light Password Security Game* and singing *The Silly Password Song*. Chapter 3 keeps the fun going, with data and analysis using Robot Dance Parties and graphing (and maybe eating!) M&M's (or your preferred treat).

Reference

Lau, W. (2020). *Computer Science Colouring Book: A Gentle and Fun Introduction to Computer Science*. William Lau.

Chapter 3

Data and Analysis

Introduction

Teach your learners to enjoy **data** analysis by incorporating fun activities such as Robot Dance Parties and graphing (and perhaps eating) M&M's (or your preferred treat). Use the lessons in this chapter to teach the difference between digital and physical (or live data), advantages and uses for each, how to make predictions, and **the Scientific Method**.

Data and Analysis—Storage—Abstraction

CSTA K-2 Standard 1A-DA-05: Store, copy, search, retrieve, modify, and delete information using a computing device and define the information stored as data.

"All information stored and processed by a computing device is referred to as data. Data can be images, text documents, audio files, software programs or apps, video files, etc. As students use software to complete tasks on a computing device, they will be manipulating data."

When kids are first learning about data, they will need to be explicitly taught what to call different types of data, how to differentiate between types of data, and how to save and retrieve files. When starting these topics with your youngest learners, it's useful to connect the digital world to tangible, physical objects that they can touch and manipulate, whenever possible.

For example, consider having a printed and digital copy of the same photo, a digital and printed written document, and a microphone that you can speak into live and then record your voice digitally to play back. When comparing and contrasting these, it's also useful to explain when it's helpful to have a digital vs. a physical (or live) representation of the data (and vice versa).

Activity: Compare and Contrast Digital Data vs. Physical/Live Data

Prepare your data and tangible objects in advance:

- Digital and physical copies of the same photograph.

- A microphone (this can be the one built into your device) and some sort of recording software, ready to record your voice—Voice Memo, Voice Recorder, or web-based Vocaroo (https://vocaroo.com) would all work well.

- A physical and digital copy of a document. This could just be a list of the names of your learners, a written sentence or paragraph (in Microsoft Word, Google Docs. or whatever works best for you) with printed copies.

DOI: 10.4324/9781003501503-3

Or if you want to get fancy, you could make an invitation for something fun (a field trip, a party) that you design. Canva (www.canva.com) is one of my favorite tools to use for designing invitations.

These data comparisons can be done all at once, or you could address them one at a time over the course of several days—whatever works best for you and your learners.

Script for Comparing Digital Photo Data vs. Physical Photo Data

Hand a physical photo out to your learners and display the same digital version of the photo on a device so that it's visible to all. Ask them to name what they notice that's the same and what they notice that's different between the digital and printed photo. Listen to their responses and clarify any misconceptions. Tell them that the photo is a type of data that you can see.

Differentiate and name the physical and digital copies. Ask them what they think the advantages of having each type are: "What can I do with this [point] physical photo that I can't do with this [point] digital photo" (and vice versa). Guide the conversation to help your learners think about photo manipulation and reproduction with the digital version. Contrast that with how the printed copy will be accessible all the time, whereas the digital copy could require batteries/power or maybe an Internet connection, depending on how it's stored/saved.

Script for Comparing Live Audio Data vs. Recorded Audio Data

Open up your preferred voice recording software, so that's ready to go. Voice Memo, Voice Recorder, or web-based Vocaroo (https://vocaroo.com) would all work well. Because Vocaroo is web-based and therefore available on any device with an Internet connection, this script will use Vocaroo as the example.

Say a sentence out loud to your learners without recording it—for example: "I'm super excited to teach you about computer science today! I'm so glad you're all here. I'm telling you this out loud because I want you to hear it, live. Is there a way I could save this message as recorded data, so you can hear it again later? Even if I'm not here?" Give your learners a chance to respond.

Next, open up your audio recording software. Narrate to your learners what you're doing. For example: "I'm opening up this audio recording software right now. I'm going to use it to record my voice. Voice recordings, just like photos, are a type of data. The software I'm using to create this audio [point to your ear] data is called Vocaroo. Can you repeat that back to me? You can access Vocaroo with any device that has an Internet connection. You just type Vocaroo into a **search engine** like Google, or type in the **URL**, vocaroo.com. I'm going to use it to record my voice in just a moment. See the red microphone icon [point to it on the screen]? When I'm ready, I just click on that and start talking. Make sure to turn *your voices* off, so only my voice is getting recorded *this time*. Ready? 3-2-1 voices off."

"I'm clicking on the red microphone to start my recording...now [click on the red microphone icon]...I'm super excited to teach you about computer science today! I'm so glad you're all here [press the red square icon in the center to stop you're recording]. While Vocaroo was recording my voice, it showed me a flashing red square within a square. Did you see that? Did you notice that I clicked that big red box (within a box), in the center to stop and save my recording? What else did you notice on my screen? Let's start our recording over by clicking on this refresh button on the left [click on the red circle with the arrow icon] and look again. Notice that doing this will *erase* the first recording. I'll show you how to *save* your recording in a moment."

Figure 3.1   Image of the recording button on the Vocaroo website.

Click the red refresh button and point out the seconds counter to the right of the recording button, and the pause button to the left. Explain that the seconds counter tells you how long your recording is (in seconds), and the box with two lines, on the left of the screen, is the pause button. The pause button is used to pause your recording if you want to take a break; you can then click it again to continue that *same recording* when you're ready.

Figure 3.2   Image of a recording in progress on the Vocaroo website.

If you're working with older learners, you may want to stop here and give them the opportunity to try recording their own voices. You'll want to make sure they can get to Vocaroo easily on their devices. Have "Vocaroo" written on the board or share the link through a **learning management system** (LMS).

Lastly, you'll want to make sure to explain to your learners how to save and share their voice recordings/audio data. Direct them to the green rectangular box icon that says "Save & Share" on the bottom of the screen and tell them to click on that once they've got a recording that they like.

Figure 3.3   Image of the save & share screen on the Vocaroo website.

This will give them several options including copying the link to the recording (so that they can paste it into your LMS to turn in), emailing it, downloading it as an .MP3 file, creating and saving a **QR code** to access it, and more. Direct your learners to the option that works best for them.

Figure 3.4   Image of the additional sharing options on the Vocaroo website.

Conclude this lesson by repeating your initial statement: "I'm super excited to teach you about computer science today! I'm so glad you're all here. I've said this out loud to you, and now I've recorded it too, because I really want you to hear that message, how glad I am that you're here with me today! In this lesson we learned about data. What's the difference between when I spoke that sentence to you *without* recording it versus when I recorded it?" Give your learners a chance to respond, then continue: "What are some things that I can do with the audio recording that I can't do when I just speak out loud (without recording it)?"

Point out that when you say the sentence live, your learners can see your body language and facial expressions. This makes it easier for them to see how glad you are to teach them. However, the audio recording of that message can be saved and shared, which can be very useful, too—especially for sharing the recording with someone who isn't here today.

Have your learners come up with their own examples for why voice recordings are useful. If you're working one-on-one, your learner could just tell you about their ideas directly. If you're working with a big group, this is a good opportunity to "pair and share" by having your learners pair up with one or two other kids next to them, and take turns sharing their ideas with each other. To conclude this lesson, call on a few learners to share with the group. If you want to reinforce the mechanics of the lesson, you could even have them record their favorite thoughts and save and share those.

Script for Comparing Digital Document Data vs. Physical Document Data

Create an invitation. Print a copy and have a digital copy displayed in a place that your learners can easily see. Feel free to use the example below. You can access a copy of the sample invitation on my website (authorjuliedarling.com).

Greet your learners and tell them that you're super excited to invite them to a robot dance party (or whatever your invitation says). Tell them that you've created this invitation so that they can remember the details, the time and place, so that they don't miss it. Explain that this invitation is a type of data called a document.

You're Invited to a
Robot Dance Party!!!

Date:

Time:

Location:

Ask: "What can I do with this physical document? Can I hand it to you to look at? Could you draw on it or add details?" Next ask: "What about this digital copy of the invitation? Which one could I email to your grown-ups so that they can read about the robot dance party, right now? Which one could you carry home to show them?" Have your learners give their own examples of the advantages to each kind of data, the physical vs. digital invitation, and why they might choose to create it one way instead of the other (or when might it be a good idea to make both).

Consider following up this lesson with an actual robot dance party. Your learners could dress like robots and/or dance like robots. You could even create a playlist of themed songs, "The Robots", "It's More Fun to Compute," and "Home Computer" by Kraftwerk and "We Are the Robots" by Yo Gabba Gabba! Are all good choices. "Do the Funky Robot" by Bounce Patrol is also fun. You should be able to find all of these by Googling; however, I also have a selection of Robot Dance Party resources linked on my website (authorjuliedarling.com).

Data: Extension

As your learners get older and develop a good understanding of using data, point out **file extensions** (.pdf, .mp3, .docx). Explain that the file extension tells you what type of data that file contains. Understanding different types of files and file extensions is necessary for more sophisticated tasks such as uploading, downloading, and converting files.

You'll also want to talk about how data is stored and retrieved. Explain the differences between storing data on "**the cloud**" (on your Google Drive, for example), on your local drive on your school or home computer, on a shared drive, or on an external storage device. Include why you'd want to create backups of important data (just in case a file is **corrupted** or accidentally deleted).

As your learners get more skilled, it's also useful to teach them about how to organize data so it's easily found, how to use logical naming conventions, and why saving groups of data in folders is useful. For example, while writing these books, I saved each book in a separate folder. The folder and manuscript for *Little Computer Scientists* were called "Little Computer Scientists" and although I kept earlier versions of the manuscript, I named each version with a number (*v.7 Little Computer Scientists*, for example), so that I could easily find the most recent version. Organizing and naming data can transfer into other computer science skills too—web design, for example.

HTML/Web Design: First Steps

When designing websites, the web designer needs to figure out which links to add to the navigation menu and/or sidebar, what to name them, and how to organize those linked pages, so that people can locate them easily. This coupled with an understanding of **HTML** and **CSS** (and perhaps **JavaScript**) can develop into a web design career.

Google Sites is an easy, free place for kids to practice HTML basics. Google Sites is connected to your Google account. Choose a new blank site, so it's easier to see what you've made. In order to practice using HTML, locate the right-hand navigation where it says "Insert". From here, you can access "Embed". Choose "Embed code", type in your HTML, then click "Insert" in the bottom left corner.

Figure 3.5   A Google Sites screenshot demonstrating where HTML can be hand entered.

There are a plethora of book and online resources for learning HTML. For young learners just starting out, I like the "HTML with the Caveman" videos from SuperCampus Jr (www.youtube.com/@supercampusjr9058).

Data and Analysis—Collection and Visualization and Transformation—Communicating, Abstraction

CSTA K-2 Standard 1A-DA-06: Collect and present the same data in various visual formats.

"The collection and use of data about the world around them is a routine part of life and influences how people live. Students could collect data on the weather, such as sunny days versus rainy days, the temperature at the beginning of the school day and end of the school day, or the inches of rain over the course of a storm. Students could count the number of pieces of each color of candy in a bag of candy, such as Skittles or M&M's. Students could create surveys of things that interest them, such as favorite foods, pets, or TV shows, and collect answers to their surveys from their peers and others. The data collected could then be organized into two or more visualizations, such as a bar graph, pie chart, or pictograph."

Activity: Use "Fun Size" Candy to Teach Kids to Graph Data

Teaching kids to analyze data using "fun size" bags of Skittles or M&M's is my favorite way to teach this skill because it's *extremely* engaging for kids. However, before you even introduce this lesson, you'll want to make sure that your learners understand that they *cannot* eat the candy until they've *completed* the analysis (and maybe even shown the results to you, too). If your learners are anything like mine, you'll need to repeat this direction several times before handing out the candy, and perhaps have them repeat it back to you: "When can you eat your candy?" (Not until the end when you say it's okay).

When to Teach This

This activity requires a basic understanding of counting, writing, or typing numbers (1–10) and identifying and writing or typing the names of colors. This would likely work well starting at the mid-point or end of Kindergarten (around age 5½). Older learners also find this engaging and could create more sophisticated graphs with their data using Excel or Google Sheets.

To Scaffold in Advance

If you're working with younger learners, scaffold this part by providing a word bank with the names of the colors found in the "fun size" candy of your choice, written someplace easily viewable, or feel free to copy the *Use "Fun Size" M&M's to Create a Bar Graph* handout. Consider writing the names of the colors using *those colors*. For example, write "green" in green, "red" in red, etc. to assist with word recognition.

It's also useful to have a number line either at the desk/work station(s) or posted on the wall that your learners can consult as they count their candies.

Note that food activities can sometimes be problematic. Before buying the candy, make sure you're not going to run into allergen issues. If food allergies or other dietary restrictions are a problem, consider doing this activity with colorful beads or something similar.

Gather Your Materials

For this activity you'll need:

- One "fun size" bag of candy for each learner.

- One piece of graphing paper, one piece of plain paper (or two pieces of plain paper if you don't have graphing paper) or the *Use "Fun Size" M&M's to Create a Bar Graph* handout.

- A pencil for each learner and drawing tools (crayons, colored pencils, or markers) in colors corresponding to the candy colors (blue, brown, green, orange, red, yellow).

- A word bank of the candy colors (for younger learners) written in the corresponding colors.

- A number line (for younger learners, optional).

- A ruler if your learners will be creating graphs on plain paper (optional).

- Devices with software for graphing your digital data (for older learners).

Script for Teaching

Hand out one "fun size" candy pack to each learner and remind your learners again that they should not eat the candy until the activity is done. Hand out the papers and tell them that they can open up their candy and dump it out on top. Instruct your learners to group the candy into piles, by color. Once the candies have been separated by color, have them write the name of the color next to each pile (they could write these color names using the color, if they wished—for example, "green" using a green colored pencil). If you're using the *Use "Fun Size" M&M's to Create a Bar Graph* handout, you can skip the step of writing down the names of the colors (but your learners could still color the words with the corresponding color, if learning colors is a skill they're working on).

Next, have them count how many candies they have in each color pile. Demonstrate this by telling your learners to count the first pile, write the number of candies on the paper next to the name of the color, then count that *same pile* a second time to check their work. If they get a different count the second time, have them check again. They could also work with a friend to check each other's work.

Once they're confident that their count is correct, they can draw a bar graph (or use the one on the handout) and color in the number of boxes that correlate to the number of candies in each color. For example, if they have three red M&M's, they should color (using red) in the row labeled "red" columns 1, 2, and 3. Have them repeat this process until they've graphed all of their M&M's.

Use "Fun Size" M&M's to Create a Bar Graph

Name _____

Open your "Fun Size" packet of M&M's but don't eat them—yet!

Organize your candies into piles by color. How many of each color do you have?

Count Your M&M's

Color	Number of M&M's
Blue	
Brown	
Green	
Orange	
Red	
Yellow	

Once you've figured out how many of each are in your packet, use the bar graph below (by coloring in the rectangles) to show how many of each color were in your packet by coloring in the boxes up to the number. Label the numbers columns "Number of M&M's"; label the colors rows "Color of M&M's".

Graph Your M&M's

	1	2	3	4	5	6	7	8	9	10	11	12	13	14	15	16	17	18	19	20
Blue																				
Brown																				
Green																				
Orange																				
Red																				
Yellow																				

Extension Activity: Make a Digital Graph of Your Data

If you're working with older learners, you can use the data collected on their papers to create digital bar graphs and pie charts using Excel or Google Sheets (or whatever works best for you) to display the results. If you're working with a group, they could also compare their numbers and maybe even find the mean, medium, and average number of each color.

To create a pie chart with the data in Google Sheets, have your learners do the following:

1. Navigate to a Google Sheets shortcut or start a new Google Sheet from their Google Drive by going to +New and selecting "Google Sheets" from the drop-down menu.

2. Give the new Google Sheet a title in the top-left corner, so their Google Sheet is easy to locate in their Google Drive (just in case they close it by accident or need to find it later).

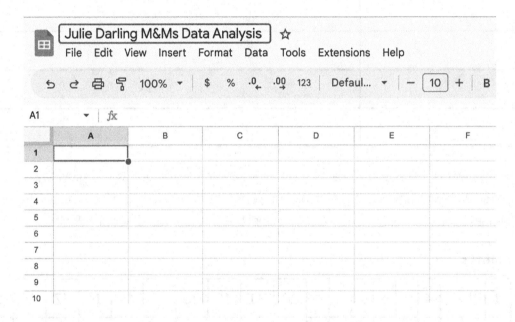

Figure 3.6   An example of how to name a Google Sheet so it can be located easily.

3. Have your learners use the physical paper document they used before (to write out the numbers and colors of the M&M's in their "fun size" pack) to label and fill out these corresponding columns in their Google Sheet.

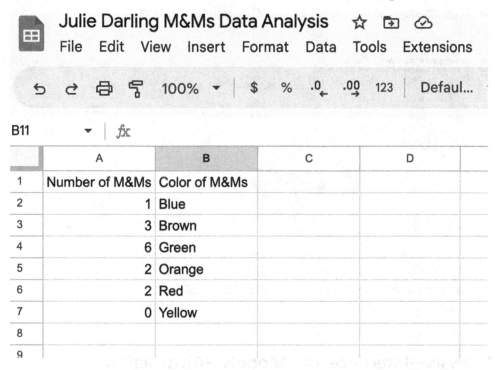

Figure 3.7   An example of how to add the M&M's number and color data to a Google Sheet.

4. Next, have them click and drag to select the data they'd like displayed on their pie chart. Then from the top-bar navigation click "Insert" and select "Chart".

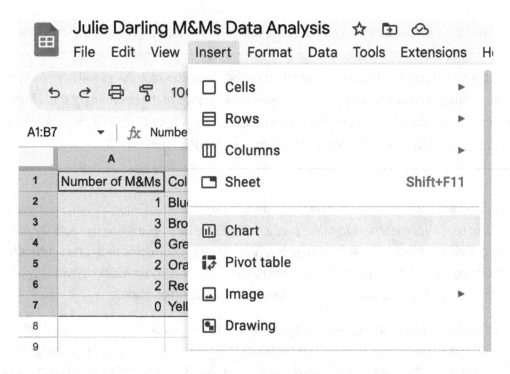

Figure 3.8   A screenshot selecting the data and inserting a chart in Google Sheets.

5. A pie chart is the default. It will display along with the chart editor tool in the far-right side of the screen. Under the "chart type" drop-down in the chart editor, your learners can choose to display the data as a different chart type, change the label, or perform other edits as desired.

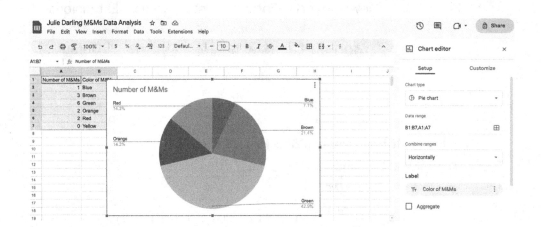

Figure 3.9   A pie chart of the M&M's data created with Google Sheets.

Data and Analysis—Inference and Models—Abstraction

CSTA K-2 Standard 1A-DA-07: Identify and describe patterns in data visualizations, such as charts or graphs, to make predictions.

"Data can be used to make inferences or predictions about the world. Students could analyze a graph or pie chart of the colors in a bag of candy or the averages for colors in multiple bags of candy, identify the patterns for which colors are most and least represented, and then make a prediction as to which colors will have most and least in a new bag of candy. Students could analyze graphs of temperatures taken at the beginning of the school day and end of the school day, identify the patterns of when temperatures rise and fall, and predict if they think the temperature will rise or fall at a particular time of the day, based on the pattern observed."

To address this standard, leverage the *Use "Fun Size" Candy to Teach Kids to Graph* data from the activity in the previous section, to teach your learners to make predictions. Have them complete the activity a second time, but *before opening their candy packets*, have them guess how many of each color they predict that they'll find in their packet. They could write these predictions down individually, or if you're working with a group, you could call on one learner for each color prediction. Have them explain their reasoning.

Ask your learners to figure out a way to make their predictions more accurate. For example, rather than just guess, perhaps they could consult with other kids and compare their results. If you're working one-on-one with your learner, you both could eat *a lot* of M&M's and keep data for each packet (you could also just count them without eating them and save the eating for later, which is less exciting but may be better for preventing a tummy ache).

If you're working with a group, a more precise method would be to tally the results from everyone who participated in the first round, tally the average of each color found from the group results, and use this to make your predictions. Once they've crunched the actual numbers, your learners can compare these to their predictions. These steps; asking questions, doing research, making a prediction/hypothesis and testing that hypothesis are the steps in **the Scientific Method.** After the hard work of predicting, tallying, comparing, and analyzing, celebrate with an M&M's eating party. Consider playing selections from the album *Here Come the 123s* by They Might Be Giants, while your learners enjoy their M&M's.

Conclusion

I hope Chapter 3 has inspired you to have an amazing Robot Dance Party, with bellies full of M&M's (or other treats) while gazing at your lovely graphs. Perhaps it has whet your appetite for learning more about web design, recording messages (maybe even podcasts?), and using the Scientific Method. Don't stop yet! Chapter 4 delves more deeply into the backbone of computer science: the basics of **algorithms** and programming.

Chapter 4

Algorithms and Programming

Introduction

Chapter 4 digs deeply into **algorithms** and **programming**, topics at the backbone of computer science. Use this chapter to teach your learners about **decomposition**, **iteration**, **algorithms**, **sequences**, **variables**, **debugging**, **loops**, **attribution**, **binary**, and **ciphers**. Set your learners up for success by starting early with sorting, keyboarding, and pair programming. Sing *The Debugging Song* together and don't forget to write your names in "secret code" using binary!

Programming—Scaffolding and Other Considerations

Sorting

With your youngest learners, use sorting activities to reinforce pattern recognition, a crucial skill needed for programming and **debugging**. When teaching your young learners to put materials away, sort supplies into boxes and bins in different ways, with words and photographs on the front to indicate which way items should be sorted, and to support emergent reading. Switch this up periodically to help them learn different patterns/ ways of sorting.

For example, store blocks, art supplies, and other materials by numbers, blocks with numbers, number of sides, or whatever you think would work best with your materials, letters, shapes, and colors. This could be done with found objects (pine cones and leaves), as well as playroom or classroom materials. Consider structuring your learning environment this way. You can find endless suggestions and toys by Googling "Montessori sorting".

Give your learners a sense of ownership by asking *them* how objects or supplies should be sorted to make them easy to find, or easy to use, for certain activities. For example, ask your learners: "If I want to draw a picture of my house, how can I organize the drawing supplies so I can find the colors I want to use, quickly?" Making tasks quicker and easier is one of the main reasons computers are so powerful and useful. **Scaffolding** this idea with everyday tasks helps young learners start thinking this way.

Pair Programming

When teaching kids about programming, have them pair up to work on tasks. This method of learning when applied to programming is called **pair programming**. Here's how it works. Two kids will work together, frequently switching roles. One kid will start by writing the code—they're called the "driver". The other kid—the "navigator"– will check the code and give input. With younger kids, you'll want to set a timer at five-minute intervals to remind them to switch roles. As your learners get older, they'll get better at switching roles independently. When first starting pair programming, you'll need to monitor your learners to make sure they're both actively participating

DOI: 10.4324/9781003501503-

and switching roles at the designated intervals. You may also need to tell your learners who should start in which role.

Keyboarding Skills

Younger learners should start learning the concepts behind coding using block-based coding. The **ScratchJr app** is great for ages 5–7, at which point they should progress to Scratch, which was developed for ages 8–16. Once your learners have become Scratch masters, it's time to add text-based coding.

Older learners will need to understand how to type symbols on a keyboard in order to be successful with text-based coding languages. Since most students start reading more fluently at the end of first grade, this is a good skill to teach to second graders. In addition, in order for kids to be successful with text-based coding, they need to master basic typing/keyboarding skills.

Advanced typing skills such as how to type symbols (e.g., parenthesis ( ), greater-than > and less-than < signs, backslash \) and capital letters should be covered before text-based programming is attempted. Typing Club (typingclub.com) is a great, free resource to use to learn typing skills. As the adult (parent/guardian or teacher) guiding your students, you'll need to remind them to keep their fingers on the home row, so that later on they'll be able to type quickly and efficiently, without looking at their hands.

It's generally recommended to start learning text-based coding by starting with **HTML/CSS** or **Python**. See the *Resources* section of this book for recommended books and sites to use to learn these. You can also find links to these resources on my website (authorjuliedarling.com). In *Little Computer Scientists*, the characters "use Python in the command line". The **command line** is a way to type instructions directly into the computer instead of using your mouse to click and select from a drop-down menu. This text-interface often allows you to work more quickly and gives you more control over your computer. On a PC, it's accessed by locating "command prompt"; on a Mac, it's accessed by locating "terminal". Be careful with this! Because the command line gives you more control, if you make mistakes, you can really mess things up (e.g., permanently deleting important data or messing up formatting).

Algorithms and Programming—Algorithms—Abstraction

> **CSTA K-2 Standard 1A-AP-08:** Model daily processes by creating and following algorithms (sets of step-by-step instructions) to complete tasks.
>
> *"Composition is the combination of smaller tasks into more complex tasks. Students could create and follow algorithms for making simple foods, brushing their teeth, getting ready for school, participating in clean-up time."*

An **algorithm**, to put it simply, is a series of steps completed in a certain order. A great way to teach about algorithms is to teach your learners a favorite recipe. For younger learners, this could be a recipe that just requires assembly, such as trail mix. Having visual and written instructions, together, reinforces letter and word recognition for emergent readers, too.

Having the steps written out also helps to better model what algorithms in computer science look like (as opposed to simply giving oral instructions). Use this traditional trail mix recipe. Tweak for taste and allergies, and consider adding photographs of the steps, using your chosen ingredients.

Simple Trail Mix Recipe

Take out a 1-cup measuring cup and either a large reusable container, with a tight-fitting lid (that can fit four cups) or a one-gallon plastic baggie (slider or zip-style closures work best for shaking the ingredients and keeping them fresh).

Gather your ingredients:

* Raisins

* M&M's

* Peanuts (or something else crunchy)

* Cheerios cereal

Use your measuring cup to measure out one cup of each ingredient and add these (one at a time) to your container.

Seal the lid (or top of the baggie), check it to make sure it's on nice and tight, and shake vigorously to mix ingredients together. Enjoy! This trail mix is great for taking with you when you go hiking or on other adventures.

Teachers and parents/guardians can also work with younger learners to create visual/written **algorithms** to post about various routines—getting ready for bed, getting ready for school, the agenda for the school day, stations and the way that you rotate through, etc. Make sure to keep these simple—young kids can only successfully follow a few instructions at a time. No more than three at a time is a good rule of thumb (although this can be built upon as it becomes routine). Older learners can follow instructions with more steps and that have a greater level of complexity. As with all learning, find ways to make this creative and fun.

Introduce each of these routines one at a time and continue to refer to them as "algorithms"—for example, "What's our algorithm for getting ready for bed? First we brush our teeth…" Have your learner tell you what the steps are for each part of the routine/algorithm. Younger learners can point to visual steps/cues for the routines, to reinforce the steps and the order. If this feels tedious to write these all out from scratch, consider an assist from an **AI** site, such as GoblinTools (https://goblin.tools) to break your task down by steps. From there it's easy to tweak and add your own photos from school or home.

Ask your learner what would happen if you brushed your teeth *and then* put the toothpaste on your toothbrush. Discuss how the order of the steps in your algorithms/routines are important both in real life *and* when giving instructions to your computer. Doing steps in the wrong order will result in a routine/program that doesn't get your desired results.

Algorithms and Programming—Variables—Abstraction

CSTA K-2 Standard 1A-AP-09: Model the way programs store and manipulate data by using numbers or other symbols to represent information.

"Information in the real world can be represented in computer programs. Students could use thumbs up/down as representations of yes/no, use arrows when writing algorithms to represent direction, or encode and decode words using numbers, pictographs, or other symbols to represent letters or words."

Variables are a placeholder in a computer program for something that could change. This is an abstract concept that is easier for older learners to grasp. However, you can lay the groundwork and introduce vocabulary with your younger learners, too. Points/coins in video games (with the number of points/coins changing) is an example that works well for gamer kids.

Teaching Variables Using Cups and Jelly Beans

You could also demonstrate this concept with a range of ages using a cup and jelly beans. Give your learners a small cup and put five jelly beans in it. Tell your learners that your variable is 5. Tell them to choose a jelly bean (any jelly bean) and take it out of the cup (they could eat it if it's a flavor they like). Have them count how many jelly beans are left (4). Have them tell you out loud that *the variable is 4*. Repeat (maybe change it up and instruct them to eat/remove two jelly beans instead of one, etc.) until all of the jelly beans have been removed from the cup.

Begin again by adding more jelly beans (start with a different number, like 3) and repeat the process. Tell your learners: "Our variable keeps changing, but it doesn't change on its own. What is causing the variable to increase/decrease?" As your learners get older and when it's developmentally appropriate, you can make this lesson more nuanced. A good rule of thumb for when to go in depth into variables is to approach this with middle school aged students (grades 6–8).

Hopscotch Jumping Algorithm

Revisit **algorithms**/instructions on a playground with a game of hopscotch. If you don't have a hopscotch template available on a nearby playground, you can draw it with chalk. Each square should be big enough that your learner's shoe-clad foot can hop comfortably inside, but small enough that it's also possible to reach the center of the next square when hopping on one foot. A traditional hopscotch court usually looks something like this:

Pair your learners up in groups of two, or if you're working directly with your learner, you can take turns. Get something to throw into the hopscotch squares. This could be a rock, bottle cap, or whatever you have on hand. Figure out who's going first and have them throw the object into a square (in some versions of the game, you throw the object sequentially, starting in square 1, then square 2, etc.). One person hops and the other person gives the person hopping the instructions/algorithm. Only one foot is allowed in each square, and the hopper can't touch the edges. The hopper can't skip squares and once the object has been retrieved, they need to follow the squares back in reverse order with the object in their hand.

Algorithm/instructions could sound like this: "Hop your right foot into square 1, now right foot in 2, left foot in 3 at the same time" etc." The instructions have to come fast or your jumper will lose their balance (which makes it exciting)! Once the object is retrieved (often while leaning down and balancing on one foot) the person following instructions has to turn around and hop back to square 1, again without touching the outside lines of any of the squares, while still continuing to follow the numbers sequentially. If they fall or touch the outside lines (or the coaches give faulty instructions, or they don't follow the correct instructions), they can start over and try again (or give someone else a try—either rule works). Once one person has been successful, it's someone else's turn. Start with the traditional hopscotch game, then consider switching it up.

Since this game is for teaching algorithms (as opposed to traditional hopscotch), have the coach change up the algorithm/instructions. Challenge the coach to give instructions that get the hopper to the object faster, that make it less likely for them to lose their balance, or that make it more challenging. If they're really good at hopscotch, can they do it jumping backwards? The hopper should follow the instructions exactly. If the coach isn't giving correct instructions, the hopper can't be successful and they need to **debug**.

Once your learners have mastered this, consider enrolling them in a CS Fundamentals course on Code.org. This free, targeted curriculum spans ages 4–11 and includes lessons for "pre-readers". The lessons are fun and engaging, and include both online and "unplugged" options. If this platform works well for you and your learners, Code.org includes curriculum to teach computer science skills all the way through high school.

Binary

Binary is the "language" of computers. It's made up of 1s (signal on) and 0s (signal off). Computer chips are made up of transistors that act like tiny switches. If an electrical current is flowing through the transistor, it is a signal on, or 1. If no electrical current is flowing through the transistor, it is a signal off or 0. Binary is also called **machine code**. The central processing unit (CPU) of a computer can only understand information written in binary/machine code.

Since binary code is essential to computer science, it's worth teaching your learners the vocabulary and introducing the concept that something can stand for something else. In *Little Computer Scientists*, readers are encouraged to try writing their names in "secret code" using binary. Students as early as first grade (ages 5–6) can do this. Additionally, our youngest learners can "clap" in binary (open hands for 0, clap for 1). Binary can also be demonstrated by flipping a light on (1) and off (0). Make this fun by having your learners read the binary number sequence to you while you flip the light off and on, then switch roles and have them flip the switch. Use *Codes Extension Activity 2: Use Binary for Your Code* to help your learners write their name in binary. For younger learners, I find it's helpful if they circle the letters in their names first, so it's easier for them to find the binary code they want, quickly.

If you want to dig deeper into teaching kids about **codes** and **ciphers**, (and more specifically how you write secret codes by subbing out a different letter, number, or symbol for the traditional alphabet letters), it's easiest to start by simply numbering the alphabet and switching out numbers for the letters. Use *Codes Extension Activity 1: Use Numbers for Your Code* to help your young learners do just this. Another traditional option is called the Caesar (shift) cipher where you shift the letters of the alphabet (e.g., if you shift by 1 you would write A as B, B as C and so on).

Codes Extension Activity 1: Use Numbers for Your Code

Write Your Name Using Secret Code

Use the numbers below to write your name in secret code.

Start by circling the letters of your name in the key. Next, write those numbers instead of the letters of your name.

For example, Zuri would write her name:

26	21	18	9
Z	U	R	I

Write your name in secret code in the space below, using the key on the side and swapping the letters of your name out for the numbers in the key

Key
A = 1
B = 2
C = 3
D = 4
E = 5
F = 6
G = 7
H = 8
I = 9
J = 10
K = 11
L = 12
M = 13
N = 14
O = 15
P = 16
Q = 17
R = 18
S = 19
T = 20
U = 21
V = 22
W = 23
X = 24
Y = 25
Z = 26

Codes Extension Activity 2: Use Binary for Your Code

Capital Letter to Binary—Key

Letter	Binary	Letter	Binary
A	01000001	N	01001110
B	01000010	O	01001111
C	01000011	P	01010000
D	01000100	Q	01010001
E	01000101	R	01010010
F	01000110	S	01010011
G	01000111	T	01010100
H	01001000	U	01010101
I	01001001	V	01010110
J	01001010	W	01010111
K	01001011	X	01011000
L	01001100	Y	01011001
M	01001101	Z	01011010

-------   -------   -------   -------

-------   -------   -------   -------

-------   -------   -------   -------

Codes Extension Activity 3: Create a Randomized Cipher

Change the key by starting the letters of the alphabet at a different point and write your name using an *even more secure* "secret code"!

Capital Letter to Shifted Binary—Key

Letter	Binary	Letter	Binary
	01000001		01001110
	01000010		01001111
	01000011		01010000
	01000100		01010001
	01000101		01010010
	01000110		01010011
	01000111		01010100
	01001000		01010101
	01001001		01010110
	01001010		01010111
	01001011		01011000
	01001100		01011001
	01001101		01011010

-------- -------- -------- --------

-------- -------- -------- --------

-------- -------- -------- --------

Algorithms and Programming—Variables—Abstraction

CSTA K-2 Standard 1A-AP-10: Develop programs with sequences and simple loops, to express ideas or address a problem.

"Programming is used as a tool to create products that reflect a wide range of interests. Control structures specify the order in which instructions are executed within a program. Sequences are the order of instructions in a program. For example, if dialogue is not sequenced correctly when programming a simple animated story, the story will not make sense. If the commands to program a robot are not in the correct order, the robot will not complete the task desired. Loops allow for the repetition of a sequence of code multiple times. For example, in a program to show the life cycle of a butterfly, a loop could be combined with move commands to allow continual but controlled movement of the character."

One of the basic skills that young learners are taught is the sequence of a story. In school, they're read picture books or fairy tales and are asked to identify the beginning, middle, and end of the story. When given the opportunity to write (and/or draw) their own stories, kids are often given this same structure. This skill (putting events/steps in order) can be transferred to developing skills in computer science.

Teaching Sequences

In programming, the order in which the instructions are given (the **sequence**) is important to the success of the program. Revisit the tooth-brushing example from earlier (putting the toothpaste on the brush *after* brushing your teeth), or something else that your learners can make a concrete, real-life connection to.

Another scenario could be: what if your grown-up is supposed to drive you to a play date? Instead of what they normally do, they drive to the play date, then open the car door to put you in your car seat. What's the problem? What steps, in what order, does your grown-up need to take to get you to your play date? Once you've received successful answers from your learners, ask them for their own examples of problems that are created by taking steps out of order. Conclude this lesson by stating: "The order that you follow these steps is important, isn't it? In computer science we call putting steps in a certain order the *sequence*. Can you say that word back to me?"

Teaching Loops

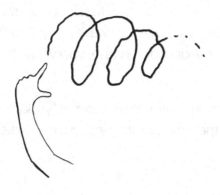

A second important concept in understanding how to write effective code is by using **loops**. Loops are a way of making your code more efficient. Instead of repeating the same line of code several times, you can simply create a loop. This is the difference between saying "Clap your hands one time, clap your hands one time, clap your hands one time, clap your hands one time" and "Clap your hands four times". You can demonstrate loops by using this example, then stating: "It's faster and easier when I just said clap your hands four times, isn't it? In computer science writing code that way is called a *loop*. Say that word back to me (loop)." If you're working with slightly older learners, you can do a check for understanding by asking them to come up with their own examples of when they could improve efficiency by using loops.

Algorithms and Programming—Modularity—Computational Problems

CSTA K-2 Standard 1A-AP-11: Decompose (break down) the steps needed to solve a problem into a precise sequence of instructions.

"Decomposition is the act of breaking down tasks into simpler tasks. Students could break down the steps needed to make a peanut butter and jelly sandwich, to brush their teeth, to draw a shape, to move a character across the screen, or to solve a level of a coding app."

Script to Introduce Decomposition

Ask your learners: "Do you like cake? Do you know how to make a cake? If you're in a classroom, ask your learners to give you a thumbs up for yes, down for no, to the side if they're not sure. Do you just snap your fingers and it's done? No! You have to know which steps to follow and in which order.

"Do you do these steps all at once? You would need SO many arms to do that. I only have two arms and I can really only handle one step at a time, even with my two arms. So, you know what I have to do? I have to break down the cake making recipe into one step at a time. Have you done that before?

"What if I miss a step or make a mistake? What would happen if I added a cup of salt to my cake instead of a cup of sugar? Give your learners a chance to respond and make sure they understand that salt instead of sugar wouldn't taste good. We need to check each step to make sure we don't make a mistake, or our cake could turn out yucky.

"Did you know that we do this with coding too? You have to take it one step at a time, and you have to check each step. With coding, checking our steps to make sure we're doing it right is called debugging. Does making a mistake when you write code mean that your code will taste yucky? No! It will mean it might not work, or maybe it doesn't work how you want it to."

To keep this lesson lighthearted, you could continue to reference "yucky code" and "yummy code". When your learners are successful, you could tell them they wrote super yummy code.

This would also be a good opportunity to show your learners how to look at code step by step by demonstrating this on ScratchJr, Scratch, or with older learners on something like Code Monster (www.crunchzilla.com/code -monster).

Another way that you can reinforce learning about **decomposition** (breaking down something into its components, like the ingredients and steps involved in making your cake) is to have your young learners look at a drawing and break it down by shapes. Use the *Learning Decomposition* handout to give your young learners some practice.

Learning Decomposition

Name _____

In the image below, write how many of the following shapes you see.

Circles _____

Triangles _____

Rectangles _____

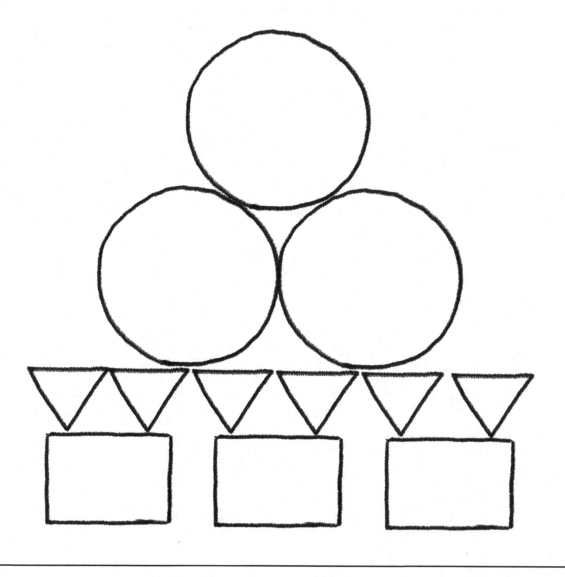

Algorithms and Programming—Program Development—Testing

CSTA K-2 Standard 1A-AP-12: Develop plans that describe a program's sequence of events, goals, and expected outcomes.

"Creating a plan for what a program will do clarifies the steps that will be needed to create a program and can be used to check if a program is correct. Students could create a planning document, such as a story map, a storyboard, or a sequential graphic organizer, to illustrate what their program will do. Students at this stage may complete the planning process with help from their teachers."

Young learners are used to working with their hands: drawing, learning to hold a pencil, and putting their thoughts down on paper. Learning how to create programs should be no different.

Encourage your learners to plan out their programs using their preferred method—this could be a storyboard, graphic organizer, or coding journal. Younger learners could draw a picture of an expected outcome. Older learners could create more details that include the sequence. Coach older learners to use notations (i.e., the multiplication symbol "×" to indicate loops) and to keep track of what worked, what didn't, and what they plan to try next.

Algorithms and Programming—Program Development—Communicating

CSTA K-2 Standard 1A-AP-13: Give attribution when using the ideas and creations of others while developing programs.

"Using computers comes with a level of responsibility. Students should credit artifacts that were created by others, such as pictures, music, and code. Credit could be given orally, if presenting their work to the class, or in writing or orally, if sharing work on a class blog or website. Proper attribution at this stage does not require a formal citation, such as in a bibliography or works cited document."

In becoming ethical technology users, even our youngest learners should be taught to give credit when using or referencing someone else's work. Start by asking young learners: "Where did you find this fantastic [name whatever it is]?" and pointing out how to find information such as author, artist, coder, or the name of the organization. If you're working with emergent readers/writers, you can have them tell you orally which work was made by which friend. For example: "Do you know who made this one? It's really important to give them credit." For learners who are progressing with reading/writing, have them practice giving credit by writing a simplified version of citing works such as "photo by Aiza", "music by Zuri", or "code by Tasha".

Reinforce this skill by asking your learners to also credit *themselves* whenever they create a unique drawing, photograph, or sentence by writing their names on their work or telling each other that they created it. You can model this live when you're showing them anything that you made, and by always crediting work made by someone else.

Continue to ask (and answer) the following questions: "*Why* should we give credit? It's the right thing to do. You want to get credit for your work, don't you? *When* should we give credit? Whenever someone has made *anything. How* do we give credit?" This last part is age dependent. Start with teaching young learners to state who made it and eventually progress (by the end of middle school) to proper citations in your preferred format. APA, MLA, or Chicago are all good choices.

Older/more advanced learners can also be taught to copy and paste the **URL** (Uniform Resource Locator, also known as a web address) for citing works found online.

As your learners get better at this, you can make finding the pieces needed for creating formal citations fun, by turning it into a scavenger hunt/race. For example, have them navigate to the same web page or open the same book and see who can locate the copyright or publication date first. Once it's found, have everyone write it down and move onto the next piece of needed information. Use the *Citations Scavenger Hunt* worksheet to gather the components needed to start creating citations. Once your learners get used to locating and gathering these pieces, the next step is to learn how to properly format the citations (consider using a citation generator such as Bibme, www.bibme.org).

Citations Scavenger Hunt—Find All the Pieces!

Book and Website Edition

Author Name:

_____

Date/Year of Publication:

_____

Title of Book or Web Page:

_____

_____

Publisher or Organization Name:

_____

_____

URL (only if it's a website or eBook):

_____

_____

Algorithms and Programming—Program Development—Testing

> **CSTA K-2 Standard 1A-AP-14:** Debug (identify and fix) errors in an algorithm or program that includes sequences and simple loops.
>
> *"Algorithms or programs may not always work correctly. Students should be able to use various strategies, such as changing the sequence of the steps, following the algorithm in a step-by-step manner, or trial and error to fix problems in algorithms and programs."*

Young learners likely aren't familiar with the term "**debug**". Consider introducing this vocabulary with a fun chant/song.

The Debugging Song

Introduce the concept of debugging to your learners with this call-and-response, "repeat after me" song. Start by telling your learners: "This is a 'repeat after me' song" and have them say that back.

Note: words can be sung or spoken depending on your preference.

You: "Quit bugging me" (slap your thigh)
Kids: "Quit bugging me" (kids slap their thighs)
You: "Quit bugging me" (slap your thigh)
Kids: "Quit bugging me" (kids slap their thighs)

You: "We've got to debug" (brush off each shoulder as you say this)
Kids: "We've got to debug" (kids brush off each shoulder)
You: "We've got to debug" (brush off each shoulder as you say this)
Kids: "We've got to debug" (kids brush off each shoulder)

You: "We've got to find the problem" (bring your hand up to your forehead, above your eyes, like you're searching for something)

Kids: "We've got to find the problem" (kids repeat gesture)

You: "We've got to find the problem" (bring your hand up to your forehead, above your eyes, as if you're searching for something)

Kids: "We've got to find the problem" (kids repeat gesture)

You: "We've got to debug" (brush off each shoulder as you say this)

Kids: "We've got to debug" (kids brush off each shoulder)

You: "We've got to debug" (brush off each shoulder as you say this)

Kids: "We've got to debug" (kids brush off each shoulder)

You: "We've got to fix the error" (pretend you're typing in the air)

Kids: "We've got to fix the error" (kids repeat gesture)

You: "We've got to fix the error" (pretend you're typing in the air)

Kids: "We've got to fix the error" (kids repeat gesture)

You: "We've got to debug" (brush off each shoulder as you say this)

Kids: "We've got to debug" (kids brush off each shoulder)

You: "We've got to debug" (brush off each shoulder as you say this)

Kids: "We've got to debug" (kids brush off each shoulder)

You: "Now our program is working!" (pump your fist in the air)

Kids: "Now our program is working!" (kids repeat gesture)

You: "Now our program is working!" (pump your fist in the air)

Kids: "Now our program is working!" (kids repeat gesture)

You: "Because we debugged" (brush off each shoulder as you say this)

Kids: "Because we debugged" (kids brush off each shoulder)

You: "Because we debugged" (brush off each shoulder as you say this)

Kids: "Because we debugged" (kids brush off each shoulder)

Script to Teach About Debugging

Once your learners are familiar with the vocabulary from this song, give them a little more context for what debugging means by explaining the origin of the term. Admiral Grace Hopper made the term "debugging" famous when she was working with a team trying to figure out why their computer was delivering errors. When they opened up the hardware, they found a moth stuck inside. The moth was causing errors! Once they removed the moth and literally "debugged" their computer, they were able to fix the problem (National Geographic, 2020).

Ask your learners: "Every time you have a problem with your computer, is it because there's a moth inside of it? What do you think?" Tell them respond with a thumbs up for yes, thumbs down for no, thumbs to the side if they aren't sure. "No, that's just what we call it now; we call computer problems bugs in honor of that moth. Debugging means that we are finding and fixing the problem."

Finally, give your learners some live examples of finding and fixing errors, debugging code. Code Monster (www .crunchzilla.com/code-monster) is a great tool to use for this. As you follow the tutorial, you can purposely make a mistake and let your learners help you find and fix it. You could also read them *Little Computer Scientists* to reinforce this skill.

Algorithms and Programming—Program Development—Communicating

CSTA K-2 Standard 1A-AP-15: Using correct terminology, describe steps taken and choices made during the iterative process of program development.

"At this stage, students should be able to talk or write about the goals and expected outcomes of the programs they create and the choices that they made when creating programs. This could be done using coding journals, discussions with a teacher, class presentations, or blogs."

Script for Teaching the Iterative Process

Ask: "When you first do something, do you always get it right that first time? (No!) Of course not. You have to practice, try different things, practice in different ways. For example, have you ever put together a puzzle? Do you have different strategies for finding which pieces fit together? What do you do if you think a puzzle piece goes in one spot, but it doesn't fit? Do you throw it on the ground and cry? (No!) You try a different spot, or if you're getting frustrated, you take a short break and come back to it later, right? This is what you do when your code doesn't work too.

"Trying different things and making changes until you get it right (or make it better) is called **iteration**. That's a big word. Can you say that back to me?" Give a demo: "This doesn't work the way I want it to, I'm going to try something else—what's that big word I used again (iteration)?" "Right! I'm going to try a new iteration to see if it works better. I'm experimenting!

It's like creating a rough draft, then working on it more, to make it better. When you're trying these different iterations, keep track of what you tried, what worked (and what didn't) in a journal. We could share what we tried to our class as a group, or (especially if we're learning from home) we could create a blog or a video to help others learn from our iterations/experiments!"

Destigmatizing Mistakes Encourages Growth

Iteration is incredibly important because it helps to destigmatize mistakes. It's not a bad thing to fail or make a mistake. Normalize mistakes, and take the stigma out, by calling them iterations. This helps kids feel safer about taking more risks, which leads to innovation (and a growth mindset). Teach kids that when they have a goal and they try something new, they should think about whether that choice got them closer or further away from their goal. If it pushed them further away, did they discover something interesting? Do they want to stick with their original goal or change it up? Celebrate students taking risks and getting outside of their comfort zones.

Conclusion

I hope you and your learners enjoyed singing *The Debugging Song*, wrote lots of secret codes using binary, and found all the parts of the citation using the scavenger hunt. I hope you utilized algorithms to both make delicious trail mix and navigate a hopscotch court. I hope you used iterations to take risks and improve or discover new things. Most importantly, I hope you and your learners had fun. Now that you understand the basics of algorithms and programming, it's time to address some of the *Impacts of Computing*. In our final chapter, we'll cover some of these impacts including online safety, **digital citizenship**, and **cyberbullying**.

Reference

National Geographic Society. (2022, May 20). Sep 9, 1947 CE: World's First Computer Bug. https://education.nationalgeographic.org/resource/worlds-first-computer-bug

Chapter 5

Impacts of Computing

Introduction

This final chapter of our book covers some of the impacts of computing. Chapter 5 discusses cyberbullying and explains the difference between being an **upstander** and a **bystander**. Details about how to create an *Old Technology Petting Zoo* and the opportunity to imagine new technology are both included, too. Use this chapter to get kids thinking about how technology has evolved and where it could go in the future. Don't forget to teach them how to be good digital citizens as they are exploring, dreaming, and inventing.

Impacts of Computing—Culture—Communicating

CSTA K-2 Standard 1A-IC-16: Compare how people live and work before and after the implementation or adoption of new computing technology.

"Computing technology has positively and negatively changed the way people live and work. In the past, if students wanted to read about a topic, they needed access to a library to find a book about it. Today, students can view and read information on the Internet about a topic or they can download e-books about it directly to a device. Such information may be available in more than one language and could be read to a student, allowing for great accessibility."

Script for Teaching About the Impacts of Computing

Start by asking your learners if their grown-ups have devices and what they use them for. Ask kids to also name what they use their own devices for. Document their responses and, depending on what they come up with, ask them a few guiding questions: "Do your grown-ups use their phones to figure out directions to places? What about the Internet—do they ever Google the answer to questions? Do they send emails to people?" Younger learners may not know, but older learners are likely aware that these uses are prolific and helpful. Next, ask your learners what happens if devices aren't working. What if the Wi-Fi goes out, the power is down, or the phone dies? What happens to the directions, emails, shows, and games?

Ask your learners: "Did you know that for most of human existence, none of these devices existed? What do you think humans did before phones? How about before the Internet? Before television shows and movies? What would you do if these things disappeared?"

DOI: 10.4324/9781003501503-

The Impacts of Technology

Tell your learners: "Now that you have some idea about how powerful computers and the Internet are (and really this *is* what a smartphone is—a computer that can fit in your pocket), what kind of programs, robots or technology could you invent? I'd love to have a robot that could clean my whole house, an app that can instantly translate books and papers written in any language, a teleportation machine, and a flying car of course! Who doesn't want a flying car?!

This would be a great opportunity to introduce some new and emerging technology such as **virtual reality**, **artificial intelligence (A.I.)**, or **augmented reality**.

Pick one to give a brief overview (see the Glossary if you need the basics) and ask your learners to think about the ways in which these could impact learning and our day-to-day lives. Can you use virtual reality to see what life is like in other countries? During historical times? What about on other planets? Yes to all of these! How about A.I.? What happens when computers are taught how to learn? Can they take people's jobs? Sometimes. Do they do as good a job as humans? Not always, but sometimes they do an even better job. Can they be used to improve our daily lives? Often in some way. Think about what you might want to teach a computer or robot to do. That's at the heart of AI. Finally, consider augmented reality. What could you superimpose into the real world, using devices, to enrich it and make it more interesting or educational?

Have your learners use the *Extension Activity: Invent New Technology* to think about a new technology they could invent. If you have the time and supplies, you could even encourage them to build a model out of cardboard, blocks, or something else. When it's finished, have them tell other people about their amazing invention or through a digital means, maybe using an online collaborative tool!

Sharing work through online collaborative tools or learning management systems is useful for a variety of reasons. These tools allow kids to share work they feel proud of and to collaborate with others. This includes collaborating with kids who may live far away and might provide diverse perspectives. This is powerful and should be encouraged. With young learners, this could mean sharing a photo of a work they've created with a family member, using **Seesaw**. With older learners, it could mean connecting with an authentic audience, through a website, video post, blog post, or podcast, about an issue that's important to them.

Extension Activity: Invent New Technology

Name _____

Invent an app, program, or other new type of technology that doesn't exist yet!

What does your technology do?

_____

_____

_____

How does it make people's lives better?

_____

_____

_____

What does it look like? Draw a sketch in the space below. Label it with details about what each part does.

Script to Discuss the Drawbacks of Technology

Ask your learners: "Now that we've discussed how cool computers and technology can be, are there any drawbacks? Do you think people talk more or less to each other in real life, when they have the option to use devices to watch shows and play games? Do you think that's a good or bad thing? Did you know that too much time on devices can sometimes make your eyes hurt? What are some fun activities that you can do when you need a break from technology? Perhaps go outside, play with blocks, do a puzzle, or read a (physical) book?"

Extension Activity: Old Technology Petting Zoo

If you really want to expand upon this topic, consider hosting an "Old Technology Petting Zoo". Although it takes a lot of preparation, this is an incredibly fun and powerful way to give your learners a chance to experience the progression of technology. You could try to show multiple technologies or just one to start with. This could always be expanded upon later.

If you want something a bit less labor intensive, compare writing with a pencil, typing on a typewriter, or using a device/computer to write something with your hands or your voice (voice to text). Ask your learners how they could send these written messages to someone far away.

If you have more lead time, consider showing kids ways in which listening to music has evolved. You could borrow or perhaps even buy if you can find them inexpensively at yard sales or thrift stores, items such as a record player, Walkman, portable CD player, boom box, radio, different generations of iPods, and a device with a streaming service such as Spotify. (Maybe you can even get your hands on an 8-track player or Victrola, or if not, show a video of these). This lesson is super powerful if you can find these in working condition, and your learners can actually listen to (age-appropriate) music. Conclude the activity by comparing and contrasting ways in which these music playing devices can be used and the music can be shared.

Some Ideas for Comparing and Contrasting Technology for Playing Music

Ask questions such as: "Could you share music with friends? What about friends who live far away? You can easily do this with music-streaming services such as Spotify, *but* you and your friend both have to subscribe to that service. People used to burn CDs and make "mix tapes" (a mix of songs on cassette tapes), but most people had less access to artists and songs than you can find now on streaming services. There's also a storage issue with older technology. You would have to store all of your cassettes, CDs, and/or records somewhere in your home."

If you have a worn-out cassette tape, you could use this to talk about how physical ways to store music can break or wear out (this is another chance to revisit storing data—in this case, music in the cloud). You could even show your learners what happens if the tape from a cassette is pulled out, how you can use a pencil to try winding it back into the cassette tape case, and that this doesn't always fix it. Point out that the advantage to physical means of storing music is that you own the CD or record forever, as long as you have space to store it and it doesn't get damaged. Contrast this with having to pay for a streaming service every month for continued access to the music you want to listen to.

Impacts of Computing—Social Interactions—Collaboration

CSTA K-2 Standard 1A-IC-17: Work respectfully and responsibly with others online.

"Online communication facilitates positive interactions, such as sharing ideas with many people, but the public and anonymous nature of online communication also allows intimidating and inappropriate behavior in the form of cyberbullying. Students could share their work on blogs or in other collaborative spaces online, taking care to avoid sharing information that is inappropriate or that could personally identify them to others. Students could provide feedback to others on their work in a kind and respectful manner and could tell an adult if others are sharing things they should not share or are treating others in an unkind or disrespectful manner on online collaborative spaces."

Digital citizenship is important to teach concurrently with computer science skills and includes being safe, responsible, kind, and respectful online. Use the same terminology that you use with your learners when teaching these skills face to face. In my classroom, I've simplified this to two basic rules. In all things we strive to be *kind* and *gentle*.

Any action that isn't kind or gentle will garner redirection or, possibly, an alternative way of accessing the content. For example, if someone can't be gentle with the computer (or when an older learner is playing an online game instead of working on the given assignment), they'll be given an "unplugged" alternative version of the activity.

Once I see that they've mastered the expectation of being kind and gentle, by telling me *and* showing me what that means, they get the chance to choose between the online and "unplugged" activity. Learners (with my help) continue to work at consistently meeting the expectation of treating ourselves, each other, and the equipment with kind and gentle words and actions.

You can follow those general guidelines too, but I'd recommend also using Common Sense Education (www .commonsense.org/education).

Common Sense Education has great, free, age-appropriate resources that can be used to teach digital citizenship and Internet safety skills. These include lesson plans, videos, and more. Start with these, but don't stop there. Once your learners have been introduced to the basic concepts and terminology, continue to address these skills as they directly apply to each lesson, using that touchstone of acting kind and gentle in all ways.

Online Safety

At each level, learners should be taught to avoid sharing the following with strangers: their full names, personal emails, physical addresses, phone numbers, the school they attend, and the city they live in. Many schools have a Safety Patrol program, where older kids help younger kids with navigating crosswalks, getting to buses, and generally staying safe. In addition to regular instruction from teachers and parents, it would also be useful to develop an Online Safety Patrol where older kids help to mentor younger kids about what information they need to keep safe and remind them how to be kind online, too.

Digital Citizenship and Cyberbullying

As online interactions, collaborations (including Internet-based gaming), and, later, social media use intensifies, continuing to reinforce to kids how to spot when someone is being unsafe or unkind online, and what to do about it, becomes increasingly important.

As anyone who has ever read online comments knows, people become more emboldened when interacting digitally. Anonymity and the perceived distance provided by digital communication make some people downright cruel. **Cyberbullying** is rampant online and my learners, as early as second grade, have reported witnessing it or even experiencing it directly, making it an important skill to cover (age-appropriately) with all kids.

Start by asking your learners to define cyberbullying. Young learners sometimes have trouble differentiating between cyberbullying and being rude, so you'll need to give them examples of each. Using all caps to shout at someone, although rude, *isn't* cyberbullying, but a group of people calling someone names and saying bad things about them online *is*. Another clear case of cyberbullying is when someone uses a photo or video of someone else to publicly shame or embarrass them.

For young learners, you could give an example: "What if you tripped and fell, and you felt embarrassed about it? That would feel bad, right? What if someone took a video of you tripping and falling and shared it with other people who continued to spread it? That would be much worse. That's cyberbullying."

Teach your learners to be **upstanders** instead of **bystanders**. A bystander is someone who witnesses a bullying behavior, either in person or online, and doesn't participate (but also doesn't do anything about it). An upstander, by contrast, is someone who does something to support the person being bullied. They take action and stand up for the person who's being bullied by confronting the bully or offering support in some other way. This could be something simple like checking in with the victim, listening to how the incident made them feel, and letting them know that you thought it was wrong and that you're on their side.

Impacts of Computing—Safety Law and Ethics—Communicating

CSTA K-2 Standard 1A-IC-18: Keep login information private, and log off of devices appropriately.

"People use computing technology in ways that can help or hurt themselves or others. Harmful behaviors, such as sharing private information and leaving public devices logged in should be recognized and avoided."

Revisit the lesson about passwords and login credentials from Chapter 2. Once your learners have mastered logging *into* (or signing *into*) their devices and accounts, it's important to teach them to log *out* (or sign *out*) from these too. You'll need to demonstrate how to do this. Make sure to wait until they're confident logging *in* to avoid frustration.

This is, of course, a particularly important skill to teach your learners who are using shared devices, but it's also a good habit to teach everyone, since it adds a layer of security. If your learners are working on shared devices and come across a device where someone has forgotten to log themselves out, teach them to be good digital citizens by logging that person out straight away.

Conclusion

Use *Supporting the Development of Computer Science Concepts in Early Childhood* to provide your learners with a solid, comprehensive foundation in computer science from which they can continue to learn and explore! Pairing this guidebook with the companion picture books *Little Computer Scientists* and *Little Hackers* helps to build vocabulary and make additional connections to the content. If you want more, consider exploring the *Resources* section of this book. You'll find even more on my website: authorjuliedarling.com.

Why I Wrote These Books:

Early Elementary Teaching Resources and Inclusion in Computer Science

I was inspired to write this series—*Little Computer Scientists*, *Little Hackers*, and *Supporting the Development of Computer Science Concepts in Early Childhood*—because I've taught technology in the K–12 setting for more than 20 years, and although there are a host of books for teaching technology and computer science concepts for kids ages 8 and up, I've been unable to find good, comprehensive books for teaching these concepts to early elementary kids. It is my sincerest hope that you've found that here.

In addition, despite all of the resources and initiatives aimed at capturing the interest of those identifying as female and **BIPOC** folks in STEM, fewer of these folks are continuing into STEM careers. In investigating why, I stumbled across a body of research indicating that part of the issue (for those identifying as female) is due to gender stereotyping. Even more troubling is that these stereotypes start as early as age 6 (Master et al., 2021). We know that representation matters, that it helps defy the stereotypes. This three-book series—*Little Computer Scientists*, *Little Hackers*, and *Supporting the Development of Computer Science Concepts in Early Childhood*—written for kids ages 4–8, is my humble contribution to help address this. I very much hope that all young learners can see themselves reflected in the pages.

Thank you so much for reading my books! You can find additional resources on my website: authorjuliedarling.com.

Reference

Master, A., Meltzoff, A., & Cheryan, S. (2021, November 22). Gender stereotypes about interests start early and cause gender disparities in computer science and engineering. *PNAS* 118(48), e2100030118. https://doi.org /10.1073/pnas.2100030118.

Glossary, Resources and Index

Glossary

This glossary includes terms in bold found throughout the text as well as other terms you may encounter when exploring computer science with your learners.

Abstraction is separating out details that aren't needed from those that are for your task at hand. Abstraction is useful for making complex ideas and concepts easier. It's zooming out and looking at the big picture instead of getting distracted by every detail. In computer science, abstraction makes it easier to understand code by focusing on core features instead of small details.

Algorithm is a set of steps done in a certain order used to complete a task or solve a problem. A recipe is an example of an algorithm.

Arrays are data structures that allow you to store a related (same data type) collection of data such as lists of numbers or names.

Artificial intelligence (AI) is when computer systems are capable of learning and problem solving. It is an emerging field of computer science. AI allows computers to perform tasks that previously only humans were capable of.

Attribution is giving credit to the author or artist of a work.

Augmented reality is when you enhance the real-world environment with virtual elements. Pokémon GO is an example of augmented reality, because the Pokémon GO characters are superimposed on your view of the real world, through your camera.

Binary is the "language" of computers. It is made up of 1's (signal on) and 0's (signal off). Computer chips are made up of transistors that act like tiny switches. If an electrical current is flowing through the transistor, it is a signal on, or 1. If no electrical current is flowing through the transistor, it is a signal off, or 0. Binary is also called "machine code". The central processing unit (CPU) of a computer can only understand information written in binary/machine code.

BIPOC stands for Black, Indigenous, and People of Color.

Blockly is a block-based visual programming language similar to Scratch.

Boolean expressions have two options "true" or "false". This could also be "yes" or "no" or "1" and "0". For example, if you're taking a quiz and you get the right answer, that would be a "true" or "yes" or "1"; if you get the wrong answer, it's "false" or "no" or "0".

Brute-force attack is when a hacker attempts to gain access to your account by trying every possible password combination. If your password is short (e.g., a four-digit number) or a word found in a dictionary, it's more vulnerable to brute-force attacks.

Bystander is a term that in digital citizenship refers to someone who witnesses someone being mean online, and although they don't participate in the unkind behavior, they also don't do anything to help.

Ciphers are a way of rearranging letters (or uses other substitutions) to disguise a message.

The Cloud refers to everything (e.g., objects, devices) that connects through the Internet. The cloud is the biggest network in the world. Using the cloud to connect your devices through the Internet is referred to as **cloud computing**.

Code refers to symbols, letters, words, and numbers that represent something else. Some examples include a secret code, Morse code, or computer code.

Coding is writing a set of instructions that a computer can understand. This is often used synonymously with programming, but programming includes design, testing, maintenance, and more.

The command line is a way to type instructions directly into the computer (instead of using your mouse to click and select from a drop-down menu). This text-interface often allows you to work more quickly and gives you more control over your computer.

Computational thinking is a set of skills for solving problems that includes decomposition, abstraction, pattern recognition, debugging, iteration and algorithmic design.

Computer science is the study of computational systems and includes computer networks, artificial intelligence, application development, video game development, and more.

Conditions (sometimes called selections) are decision-making instructions given as part of the computer program. They're essentially a coding flowchart that gives If-then instructions. For example, if it's raining (this is TRUE), then we'll have indoor recess; if it's raining (this is a FALSE—it's *not* raining), then we will play outside.

A corrupted file is a file that's been damaged or is not performing as it should.

CSS (Cascading Style Sheets) (see HTML).

Cyberbullying is when someone (or a group of people) uses a digital tool (social media, the comments section on an online site, a gaming site) to bully someone else.

Cybersecurity is the field dedicated to keeping computers and systems safe. Cybersecurity professionals are sometimes referred to as "white hat hackers" or "ethical hackers".

Data refers to all information stored and processed by a computer. This includes computer instructions, numbers (prices, quantities, measurements), text (names, addresses), images (photos, painting, drawings), audio (voice, music), and video (movies, animations).

Databases are used to effectively store and search for large amounts of data. An example of a database is the U.S. Library of Congress digital collections database, where you can locate primary source documents for historical events.

Data structures are the ways in which data are stored for easy access. These include arrays, trees, and databases.

Debugging is finding and fixing mistakes or problems in computer programs.

Decomposition is breaking something down into smaller pieces, steps, or tasks. This is a useful skill for finding solutions and problem solving. Breaking code into smaller chunks can make the code easier to understand.

Deep learning (see AI).

Digital citizenship is being safe, responsible, kind, and respectful online.

Emergent readers refers to kids who are learning to read. This could be our youngest learners who are learning to recognize the letters of the alphabet and the sounds the letters make or kids who can recognize some words but aren't yet independent readers.

File extensions are the letters at the end of a file name, following the period. These tell you what kind of file you're working with.

Functions are a way to chunk blocks of code. This makes it easy to reuse common code blocks. Grouping code together in this way also allows programmers to read, write, and debug code more quickly and easily. Some programming languages have built-in functions, which are called methods.

Hackers aren't always up to no good. There are three categories of hacking: white hat, gray hat, and black hat. **White hat hacking** is what cybersecurity experts do. They work to find and fix vulnerabilities and try to prevent other hackers from getting in. **Gray hat hacking** is when someone hacks into systems (without permission) in order to raise awareness and expose vulnerabilities (this is also called hacktivism). **Black hat hacking** is when someone hacks into a system (without permission) with the intent to do damage and/or steal information.

HTML (HyperText Markup Language) and CSS (Cascading Style Sheets) are the basic building blocks of web design. HTML is used to structure the content of web pages, CSS is used to format the content, that will then cascade through the whole page (as opposed to having to make changes on each line of code). For example, if all the title headings on your page are green and you want to change them to purple, you can use CSS to do that—quickly!

Icon/thumbnail is the tiny, clickable picture (which sometimes also includes text), that provides an idea for what the program or file is.

Internet of Things (IOT) are devices that can be controlled through the Internet. This includes computers, phones, appliances, lights, and more.

Iteration is part of the engineering design process whereby you continue to improve your design to fix problems and make improvements. This applies to improving or fixing your code.

JavaScript is a web programming language for creating dynamic/interactive website content.

Key is the tool used to encrypt or decrypt data—for example, when encoding or decoding a secret code.

LAN stands for Local Area Network This is a way of connecting devices together to form a network. It's often used to allow several people to access the same information. One intriguing use of a LAN is to set one up so that your kids can play Minecraft with their friends. As they get older, they can learn to do this themselves. Another example of a LAN is a Wi-Fi router in a house. This is a LAN that connects the devices that you use at home which could include computers, televisions, smart speakers, smart thermostats, smart appliances, etc.

Learning management system (LMS) are systems such as Google Classroom, Canvas, Blackboard, or Seesaw (a limited learning management system that's considered a better fit for early elementary-aged kids). They are tools used to organize and share resources with students, quickly and easily.

Loops are programming instructions that are repeated until a certain condition is met.

Machine code (see **Binary**).

Malware also called malicious software, is a program that's designed to cause harm. Different types of malware do different things, including slowing down your device, sending spam emails that infect other devices (viruses), stealing your personal data, or even preventing you from accessing anything on your device until you pay the hacker money (ransomware).

Micro:bit is a physical computing device, sometimes referred to as a "tiny computer".

Mouse over/mouse hover is when you move your mouse/cursor over something, but don't click. Mousing over something on a computer often results in displaying additional information before you click. This is a useful skill (and time saver) to teach to young leaners.

Multi-factor authentication is a method of making your account more secure. When this is enabled, the first "factor" is your password, the next "factor" could be a verification code that was texted or emailed to you, biometrics such as voice, fingerprint, face or retina scan, etc.

Open Source is where anyone can see the code. Anyone is also allowed to use it and edit it.

Operating systems manage all of the software and hardware running on your device. The three most commonly used operating systems are Microsoft's Windows, MacOS, and Linux.

Pair programming is when two people pair up to code together. One takes the role as the "driver" and writes the code while the other person, the "navigator", will check the code and give input. The driver and the navigator switch roles frequently.

Penetration testing also called "pen testing", is when a cybersecurity expert launches a fake cyberattack to locate vulnerabilities.

Phishing is when someone tries to trick you into giving them your information. Phishing scams are used to steal anything from passwords to bank account information. One of the most common types of phishing is to send an email that asks you to click on a link, to log into an external account. Once you click on that link, a fake account login page is opened, and you unknowingly input your login credentials into a login page that the scammer controls. Now the scammer has your credentials and account information.

Physical computing is sometimes used interchangeably with robotics as both can include devices with sensors, lights, displays, motors, and other inputs/outputs. For our purposes, I've differentiated "physical computing" as objects that have multiple pieces that can be added and/or assembled as desired.

Pop-ups are advertisements (and other messages) that pop up on your screen. Sometimes they're simply advertisements. However, one type of black hat hacking is to create a pop-up ad that tells users they have a virus on their computer and that they need to download software to clean the system. However, when they download that software, instead of cleaning the system, it installs a virus. Another common tactic is not to install a virus, but to tell the user the device is infected with malware and instruct the user to call a telephone number that the scammer answers. Then s/he will trick the user into installing software that allows the scammer to control the user's device. Lots of pop-ups suddenly appearing is often a sign that there is malware installed on your computer. When your computer is suddenly running more slowly than usual, that can also be indicative of a malware.

Programming (see Coding).

Python is a popular software coding language (named after the BBC comedy series *Monty Python's Flying Circus*). It has many applications including: artificial intelligence, machine learning, game design, creating websites and data analytics, making it quite versatile. Python is considered a "high-level" programming language, which means it's easy for people to read and write. This is part of what makes it a good programming language for beginners. In addition, you can run each line of code to check for errors, making it easier to troubleshoot. A good progression for kids learning to code is to start with ScratchJr, progress to Scratch, and then explore Python and/or HTML/CSS.

QR code is a "quick response" barcode which, when scanned, links to some sort of data or information.

Quarantined virus is a virus that has been confined to a safe area where it can't infect the rest of your device. You do this using antivirus software.

Ransomware is a type of malware that keeps you from accessing your files, unless you pay money to the malicious hacker.

Raspberry Pi is an inexpensive personal computer that can fit in the palm of your hand. There are a variety of accessories that you can connect to your Raspberry Pi. Some of these are for usability: for example, a power supply, monitor, mouse, keyboard, and micro-SD card. Some of these are for innovation: for example, a camera, or the "Sense Hat" which allows you to track your environment for variations in pressure, humidity, movement, and more, and use the built-in LEDs (light-emitting diodes, which look like little light bulbs, but are actually considered tiny semiconductors) to see this data. Python is a good language to use with a Raspberry Pi (you can also use Scratch).

Rebooting is restarting your computer.

Root (see Tree).

Safe-mode is where you start your computer with only a few items running. Safe-mode is used to diagnose issues with your computer.

Scaffolding is where you offer support when teaching kids a concept that they may have difficulty learning without the extra support. For example, you can scaffold using correct terminology by providing a word bank.

Scratch is a block-based visual programming language. Scratch is integrated into a whole community of sites and apps and was created to teach kids ages 8–16 to code.

ScratchJr app is a visual programming language that uses puzzle piece-style blocks of code to (drag and drop) to write a program. ScratchJr was designed for emergent readers ages 5–7.

The Scientific Method involves a logical progression of steps used to find the solution to a question or problem. These include asking questions, doing research, making a prediction/hypothesis, and testing that hypothesis.

Search engine is the software that allows users to search the Internet using keywords (as opposed to having to type in the exact URL). Common search engines include Google, Yahoo, Bing, and DuckDuckGo.

Sequences are a series of instructions followed in a certain order.

Snap! is block-based coding similar to Scratch. It was designed by UC Berkeley and touts "advanced features" for "serious study of computer science".

Spyware is a type of malware that runs in the background, secretly collecting sensitive data, without the user's consent.

STEM stand for Science, Technology, Engineering, and Mathematics.

STEAM stand for Science, Technology, Engineering, *Arts*, and Mathematics.

Strings are a type of data, used in programming languages, that includes letters, words, numbers, or characters. These are often enclosed in quotation marks—for example, "Hello world!" They can be used for a variety of tasks, including composing messages.

Thumbnail (see **Icon**).

Trees are a way to organize hierarchical data structures. The starting point of the tree is called a "root". For example, in web design, the root of the tree would be <html>. Everything else that comes after this is "descended from" this root.

Trojan Horse named after the ancient Greek story about the fall of the city of Troy, is when malware is disguised as a legitimate program. Once downloaded, the malware causes harm.

Upstander is a term that, in digital citizenship, refers to someone who witnesses someone being mean online, and they take action and stand up for the person who's being bullied by confronting the victim or offering support in some other way.

URL stands for Uniform Resource Locator, also known as a website address. Each web page on the Internet has its own unique URL. These usually start with http://www.

Variable(s) is a placeholder for something in a computer program that could change.

Virtual reality is a simulated 3-D experience used to make a computer-generated environment immersive. Usually, 3-D glasses or headsets are required to experience virtual reality. Some virtual reality is not recommended for kids under age 13. Younger kids are more likely to experience adverse effects such as eye strain and fatigue. Long-term research on this is not yet available, but for anyone using a VR headset, time limits are recommended.

Virus is a type of malware that modifies programs by "infecting" them with its own malicious code.

Virus scanners are part of antivirus software. When you run antivirus software, it searches through your system to locate and remove malware.

Web browser is a software application that allows you to access the Internet. Some common web browsers include Google Chrome, Firefox, Microsoft Edge, and Safari.

Wi-Fi is a system that uses radio waves to send Internet connectivity to devices, without the use of cords.

Worm is a type of malware characterized by its ability to replicate independently once it breaches a system.

Resources

Alice (www.alice.org). Free download for 3D worldbuilding. Can be used to teach the fundamentals of computer science and/or an introduction to the Java programming language. Recommended for middle school and up.

Author Julie Darling (https://authorjuliedarling.com/resources). Author Julie Darling's website for collecting resources related to computer science, makerspace, and more.

BibMe (www.bibme.org). A citation generator that can be used to format citations for bibliographies.

Bosch Best Grant (www.besteachergrant.org). The Bosch Eco and STEM teacher (BEST) grant program awards annual grants to Pre-K-12 teachers.

Canva (www.canva.com). Free, web-based graphic design tool for making invitations, posters, and more. Includes templates.

Code.org (https://code.org). Free, comprehensive computer science curriculum for K-12 educators.

Code Club (https://codeclub.org). Resources for running a Code Club for ages 9 and up. Includes free project guides for Scratch, Python, and HTML/CSS.

Code Monster by Crunchzilla (www.crunchzilla.com/code-monster). A free, web-based interactive resource for learning the basics of JavaScript.

Common Sense Education (www.commonsense.org/education). Free resources that can be used to effectively teach about Internet safety and digital citizenship in an age-appropriate way.

CS First (https://csfirst.withgoogle.com/s/en/home). Google for Education computer science curriculum. Free, web-based and includes "unplugged" activities.

Experience AI (https://experience-ai.org). Educational resources on artificial intelligence and machine learning aimed at ages 11–14.

Girls Who Code (https://girlswhocode.com). Resources for clubs (focused on girls and non-binary students but open to all) for grades 3rd–5th and 6th–12th. Also includes resources for high school summer programs and college and career computer science and technology program resources.

GoblinTools (https://goblin.tools). An AI website for breaking down tasks into steps. Describe the task, then click on the magic wand to break that task down into discrete steps. This is a perfect tool to use to teach algorithmic thinking.

Hello Ruby (www.helloruby.com/play). Free downloadable activities for learning computer science concepts.

Here come the 123s by They Might be Giants (www.theymightbegiants.com/here-come-the-123s). Fun, educational songs for children that can be used to reinforce counting and other mathematical concepts.

HTML with a Caveman (www.youtube.com/@supercampusjr9058). Silly videos from SuperCampus Jr for teaching younger learners beginning HTML.

Moon Hack (https://moonhack.com). An annual free two-week, international coding event, for ages 8–15.

Scratch (https://scratch.mit.edu). A free web-based, block-based coding site aimed at ages 8 and up.

ScratchJr (www.scratchjr.org). A free app designed to teach children ages 5–7, block-based coding.

SciGirls (https://pbskids.org/scigirls). A PBS Kids girl-focused STEM site that includes videos, games, and more.

Seesaw (seesaw.com). A communication, curriculum, and "learning management system light" tool developed with early elementary learners in mind. Used to send information between teachers, kids, and families, share lessons with kids, share work between school and home, and complete assignments. Includes a free library with computer science curriculum.

Snap! (https://snap.berkeley.edu). A free web-based, block-based coding site. Snap! is an extension/reimplementation of Scratch.

Python for Kids: A Playful Introduction to Programming by Jason R. Briggs (No Starch Press, 2022) is a comprehensive book for teaching kids Python.

Tinkercad (www.tinkercad.com). A free web-based program for 3D design, learning about circuits, and designing code blocks.

Typing Club (www.typingclub.com). A free web-based program for learning keyboarding skills.

Vocaroo (https://vocaroo.com). Free, web-based voice recording software.

Index

Printed in the United States
by Baker & Taylor Publisher Services